Deep'n as It Come

deep'n
as it come

The 1927
Mississippi River Flood

Pete Daniel

New York

Oxford
University
Press

1977

To Lisa and Laura

Acknowledgments

It would take a whole chapter to explain adequately the debts that I have accumulated in assembling this book. Raymond Smock read the manuscript, gave me numerous ideas on organization and layout, and generally encouraged the project. Leslie Rowland and Ann Weir read the manuscript and gave me suggestions on style and grammar, Caroline Taylor of Oxford University Press edited it, and David Laufer designed it. Karen Thornton helped compile the drowning statistics, and Sharon Rowlette helped transcribe some of the interviews. Leslie B. McLemore gave me hospitality and encouragement, as did Gordon Cotton and Eugene McLemore. Albert Blair, Douglas Thurman, and Bill Leary of the National Archives; Rudolf A. Clemen, Jr., of the American National Red Cross; the staff of the Herbert Hoover Presidential Library; and Leroy Bellamy, Jerry Kearns, and Milton Kaplan of the Prints and Photographs Division of the Library of Congress were especially helpful in collecting archival and photographic material. The following people and institutions aided me in locating additional manuscript and photographic material: In Mississippi, Laura D. S. Sturdivant and Clinton I. Bagley of the Mississippi Department of Archives and History; Anne G. McGuffie of the Historical Society of Vicksburg and Warren County; Henry Kline II of the Mississippi Authority for Educational Television; Hodding Carter IV of the *Delta Democrat Times;* Roger Christian and Mrs. Marie Glasco of the William Alexander Percy Library, Greenville; Barbara Griffin of the Warren County Library, Vicksburg; Birney Imes of Columbus; Newman Bolls and Gladys H. Jaudon of the Board of Mississippi Levee Commissioners, Greenville; Michael Johnson of Metcalfe; and Helena Walley and Billy Bridges of the U.S. Army Corps of Engineers, Vicksburg. In Arkansas, R. P. Baker of the Arkansas History Commission; Mrs. William Doak, Mrs. Buelah (Boots) Walker, and Mrs. Roy V. Wilson of Pine Bluff; Mrs. J. W. Jones of the Desha County Public Library, McGehee; and Anne Lee of Dumas. In Louisiana, Robert Blush of the Iberville Parish Library, Plaquemine; Danny Brown of the Louisiana Department of Public Works, Baton Rouge; Paul Coco of Marksville; Margaret Torrey and Vicky

Landry of the Iberia Parish Library, New Iberia; Carroll Martin of New Iberia; Pat Leeper of the Louisiana State Library, Baton Rouge; Lou Thomas and Anne Leggett of the Baton Rouge *State Times;* and Mrs. Rufus Yerger of Tallulah. Robert W. O'Brien of the Illinois Central Gulf Railroad furnished some photographs, and "River Rat" got me on the right track along I-40.

There were many people who gave me information about the flood whose accounts I could not use directly in this book: In Mississipi, Levye Chapple, Brodie Crump, Ignance F. Loyacono, Will B. Moore, and Ernest Sanders of Greenville; Mitchell Johnson, Charlie Person, and Bertha Ross of Metcalfe; and V. Blaine Russell of Vicksburg. In Arkansas, Mrs. J. G. Berry and Miss Cornelia Lee of Dumas; Mrs. C. A. Dawson of Marked Tree; Addie Jackson of Arkansas City; and Jim Merritt of McGehee. In Louisiana, Cy Young of Monroe. Also Robert E. Bondy of New Canaan, Connecticut, wrote to me about his role in the relief mission of the Red Cross.

The hospitality, graciousness, and helpfulness of the people of the South is legendary, as well it should be; they opened their homes, scrapbooks, and memories to me. The remainder of the book includes the words of the people who made the history; the flood left highwater marks on memories as well as on buildings and telephone poles.

This project was aided immeasurably by a National Endowment for the Humanities Summer Stipend in 1974, an American Philosophical Society Travel Grant in 1975, and a University of Tennessee Faculty Research Fellowship in 1976. I wish to give special thanks to Stella H. Daniel for her constant encouragement.

Some of the documentary material in this book comes from interviews and some from sources contemporary to 1927—newspapers, magazines, letters, official reports, reminiscences, and speeches. Though I wrote to numerous state and local libraries and historical societies asking for information and possible aid in locating people to interview, much of the oral and photographic

A Note on Interviews and Photographs

material I discovered by chance. My only other method of collecting interviews and photographs was combing the flood area as thoroughly as possible. The photographs come from varied sources, from the great and small libraries of the land, from agencies, and from the photograph albums of the people who lived through the flood.

Because most of the photographs in this book come from prints made from my own copy negatives, there is no numbered negative or print available from the repositories or people who have possession of the original photographs. In the cases where the photographs are available, the negative number is listed following the caption. The sources of the photographs are listed below.

The Red Cross collection in the Prints and Photographs Division of the Library of Congress contains an uncatalogued collection of flood photographs. Other Red Cross material, cartoons, and documents, came from the National Red Cross Headquarters in Washington, D.C., and from the Red Cross, *The Mississippi Flood Disaster of 1927* (Washington, D.C., 1928). The Herbert Hoover Presidential Library has a flood collection, as do the National Archives and the Illinois Central Gulf Railroad. In the flood area there are many excellent photograph collections: In Mississippi, the Mississippi Board of Levee Commissioners and the William A. Percy Library, Greenville; the Mississippi State Archives, Jackson; and the U.S. Corps of Engineers, the J. Mack Moore Collection in the Old Courthouse Museum, and Gordon Cotton's private collection in Vicksburg. In Arkansas, the Arkansas History Commission, Little Rock; Mrs. Buelah (Boots) Walker, and Louise N. Doak of Pine Bluff; C. D. Dupree of Watson; Desha Public Library, McGehee; and Verna Reitzammer of Arkansas City. In Louisiana, E. C. Woodyear of Mound sent me a copy of Fred P. Beneke's *The Flood of 1927*; Ed Supple of White Castle; Mrs. Rufus Yerger of Tallulah; the Louisiana Department of Public Works, Baton Rouge; the Iberville Parish Library, Plaquemine; Paul Coco of Marksville; and Myrtle Turner Staples and Carroll Martin of New Iberia.

Contents

Deep'n as It Come

1 *in the*

beginning

The waters of the earth have eternally sought their home in the seas, and streams have carved rock, eroded mountains, and flooded valleys in their search for the oceans. Eventually the rivers of the earth established their beds, and the history of civilization began to be written along the river banks of the world—the Nile, Euphrates, Tigris, Indus, and Yangtze, and, later, the Congo, Amazon, and Mississippi. People who settled along the banks of rivers adapted to the natural cycle of the waters, retreating before the floods, then advancing to the fields as the waters receded to plant crops in the fertile deposits.

Long before humans arrived along the banks of the Mississippi River its alluvial bed had been constructed from the mountain spires that rose on either side of it; they had been eroded, and the soil formed a valley ribboned with tributaries. The lower Mississippi River drank the waters from the heart of a continent. Because the banks of soft earth often crumbled into the stream, the river channel was tentative, fickle, snaking through bends and horseshoes, detouring for miles to arrive a hundred feet from where it began, and later, tiring of circumambulation, eating through the narrow strip of land to abbreviate itself. Too restless to sleep in one bed, the river for centuries had carved and re-carved the valley with its channels.

The river had its own natural cycle, usually flooding in the spring and again in early summer to carry home the spring rain and melted snow, then settling back into its bed during late summer to await a new season. For eons the river lengthened itself as it fed on soil and in flood deposited it along the banks and delta. It would drop the heavier parts of its load near the banks, and then the finer soil would precipitate across the land; thus the banks, constructed of coarser material, grew higher than the flat land beyond.

Indians called the river *Mississippi*—the Father of Waters—and for centuries they lived along its banks, moving in cycle with the rites of the river. Eventually, white explorers and, later, settlers moved along the river, discovering both the floods and the rich soil. By the eighteenth century the white men who lived near the river had learned that during mild floods they could detour the overflow past their farms by erecting small dikes, for the water would then flow past the dikes and run off into the swamps beyond, leaving the farms dry and the crops growing.

Thus, after millions of years of freedom, the river received its challenge: men attempted to alter the natural cycle of the river in flood. More and more settlers built dikes, but the longer the line they built, the more pressure the river exerted, for the surging water sought to break through. Each planter attempted to make his levee stronger than his neighbor's, but, finally tiring of this competition, planters united into organizations that worked to strengthen entire lines of levees. Then the battle was directed not against neighbors, but against the settlers on the other side of the river; as in a poker game, one side would raise and the other would call. The stakes were high, for if the levee on one bank caved in the other side would be relieved of the river's pressure. Occasionally people cheated at the game: men would destroy a levee across the river or downstream from their own farms in order to protect their crops.

During the nineteenth century the line of levees lengthened along the banks of the Mississippi, but no matter how high the levees grew in times of great floods the river would find a way through. People who lived along it came to measure time not simply in years, but in flood years—1858, 1862, 1867, 1882, 1884, 1890, 1897, 1903, 1912, 1913, 1922. The levees meanwhile grew from small dikes to large walls of earth, and local, state, and federal governments became involved in their construction and maintenance. The Mississippi River Commission, established by Congress in 1879 to work out a unified plan of flood control and navigation, cooperated with the Army Corps of Engineers to build the levees ever higher, to get them up to "grade," an arbitrary height based on the highest previous flood. The more complete the system became, however, the more pressure the river exerted on the levees—for there was no escape now from the channel, no break or spillway in the entire thousand-mile line from Cairo, Illinois, to the Gulf of Mexico.

5

The flood left its mark on music and literature. Even as the water lingered on the land, musicians began to record songs about the flood. Bessie Smith released "Back-Water Blues" in April and "Muddy Water (A Mississippi Moan)" in May. Country and western singer Vernon Dalhart recorded "The Mississippi Flood" in May, and during the same time Sippi Wallace recorded "The Flood Blues." Ernest Stoneman learned "Mighty Mississippi" from a black musician who worked for the Victor studio where he was recording. "Blind Lemon" Jefferson recorded "Rising High Water Blues" in the summer of 1927. The flood was also preserved in literature by William Faulkner in *The Old Man* and by Richard Wright in his short story, "Down by the Riverside." (Chicago *Defender*, July 2, 1927)

In 1926 the Chief of Engineers surveyed this earthen bulwark. "It may be stated that in a general way the improvement is providing a safe and adequate channel for navigation," he concluded in the *Annual Report*, "and is now in condition to prevent the destructive effects of floods." He had not been chastened by a line written almost a half-century before by a river pilot who was well acquainted with the river and its caprices. "One who knows the Mississippi will promptly aver— not aloud, but to himself—that ten thousand River Commissions, with the mines of the world at their back, cannot tame that lawless stream, cannot curb it or confine it, cannot say to it, Go here, or Go there, and make it obey; cannot save a shore which it has sentenced," Mark Twain had prophesied in *Life on the Mississippi*. With the greatest volume of water ever to run down the valley imminent, the engineers continued to assure the people of the lower valley that the levees would hold.[1]

The engineers had forgotten: the valley belongs to the river, and their dirt walls were artificial brakes on a natural cycle. As William Faulkner wrote later, the flood "was no phenomenon of a decade"; rather, the years when it did *not* flood were the phenomenon, "and the river was now doing what it liked to do, had waited patiently the ten years in order to do, as a mule will work for you ten years for the privilege of kicking you once."[2]

Nature conspired to make the spring of 1927 memorable; not only did the rivers rise, but tornadoes and earthquakes also threatened the Mississippi Valley. And for weeks it rained. The incessant downpour unnerved people along the river. As one man remembered, "It started raining, and it just never did stop." What weather expert Dr. Isaac Monroe Cline wrote about Louisiana could just as well have been said of Mississippi and Arkansas: "The flood of 1927 in Louisiana exceeded any previous flood since the settlement of this section more than 200 years ago."[3]

The flood of 1927 happened not just because of unusually heavy rains (though that was the principal cause), but also because of the cumulative tinkering of humans. Loggers for years had cut over the forests along the tributaries and the main river channel, and then farmers had cleared the land, robbing the water of a place to pause before running down to the Gulf. When the torrential rains of 1927 poured down upon the valley, the water rushed directly into the streams, and for the first time in centuries the tributaries of the Mississippi all filled and began pouring their loads into the main channel simultaneously. The river had been abnormally high all winter, and by April it was brimming over.

That mass of water had to move home to the Gulf, to sea level; there was no alternate route, no spillway, no reservoir, no break in the levee line. It had to run the gauntlet between the levees—or break them—and the higher the water in the main channel rose, the more it

7

The drainage basin of the Mississippi River covers 41 per cent of the area of the United States, including thirty-one states. (Fred D. Beneke, ed., *The Flood of 1927*, Mississippi River Flood Control Association, 1927)

backed up the tributaries. For a few days the Ohio River actually flowed upstream. Indeed, as the flooded Mississippi rolled south, the same process was repeated as the main river pushed back the already flooded tributaries. People could look up twenty feet to the levees and see the river boats floating, mirage-like, high above, as if threatening to sail over the brink. The banks were full, the levees were endangered, and the promises of the engineers became less and less assuring.

Perhaps the Army Corps of Engineers had been lulled into overconfidence by the technological accomplishments of the era. After all, aviators were continually setting flight records; several had already attempted the Atlantic, and before the flood crest reached the Gulf Lindbergh reached Paris. It was the year that Al Jolson began talking in *The Jazz Singer*, and De Hane Seagrave became the first person to drive across the earth at over 200 miles per hour. Babe Ruth hit sixty home runs that year. America exuded confidence, and doubtless the engineers were only parroting this spirit when they claimed that levees could "prevent the destructive effects of floods."

Major Donald Connolly continued to speak confidently of the levees holding till the end. On April 9 he boasted, "We are in condition to hold all the water in sight." Two days later he noted that the people of the valley "seem to have that easy confidence that the levees will hold." Two days later the press reported that Connolly "expressed deep interest in the rising waters." On April 16 confidence had begun to seep, and Connolly only said that the "situation is as well as can possibly be expected." On April 21 two major breaks in the levees occurred—at Mound Landing, Mississippi, and at Pendleton, Arkansas. For the next two months the river tore through the lower valley with the fury of a wild animal. Indeed, some observers reported that when the levees gave way and the water burst through, it *did* roar like a beast; people who heard it compared the sound to a tornado, a strong wind, Niagara Falls, a deep animal growl.[4]

Although flooding and the attendant distress affected seven states, Mississippi, Arkansas, and Louisiana bore the brunt of the flood. There was only one major break in the levee system on the east bank of the lower Mississippi River, yet that break flooded 2,323,005 acres and affected 172,770 people. An engineer estimated that as great a volume of water was pouring through the Mound Landing crevasse as passed over Niagara Falls. In Arkansas 5,104,735 acres were flooded, mainly because the Arkansas River, already filled to the brim, was pushed back by the flooding Mississippi, bursting the levees at a dozen points, from Little Rock to the main channel of the Mississippi. Arkansas also experienced two breaks in the Mississippi River levee system, four major breaks in the White River system, three in the Red River, and one in the St. Francis. To the south, a large part of Louisiana simply drowned as the water from Arkansas drained through it. When the water that had flooded the state of Mississippi re-entered the channel near Vicksburg, it broke the levee across the river at Cabin Teele, Louisiana. There 6,200,343 acres went under the flood, affecting 277,781 people. Ultimately there were forty-two major levee crevasses in the three states, and engineers counted some 120 breaks in all.[5]

From Cairo to the Gulf, about one thousand miles, the flood rolled on, sometimes spreading out to nearly one hundred miles across. In essence, the Mississippi

9

River had reclaimed its alluvial plain, and only a few levee tops, telephone poles, housetops, Indian mounds, and trees protruded above the flood. Whether one blames poor engineering, overcutting by loggers, improper contour plowing by farmers, or simply attributes it to an act of God, the Mississippi flood of 1927 marks the ultimate high water. It is a record the population of that area is anxious to see stand forever.

Statistics tell part of the story: 16,570,627 acres flooded in 170 counties in seven states, $102,562,395 in crop losses, 162,017 homes flooded, 41,487 buildings destroyed, 5934 boats used in rescue work, 325,554 people cared for in 154 Red Cross camps and 311,922 others fed by the Red Cross in private homes, and between 250 and 500 people killed. The organizations and agencies involved in rescue and relief add another dimension: the Departments of War, Navy, Treasury, Agriculture, and Commerce; the Veterans Bureau; the Red Cross; the National Guard; the U.S. Public Health Service; the Rockefeller Foundation; railroad companies; and state and local agencies.

Yet statistics and lists hang inanimate. The awesome destruction was visited upon the people who lived and worked along the river; the history of the flood is not the story of agencies or of dollars and cents, but of the experiences of each of those people in their personal struggles against the river's force and destruction.

The contradictions of sorrow and humor, helplessness and bravery, courage and fear, humility and pride, death and salvation, despair and hope, calm and panic—all reveal the human dimension of the flood disaster. As calamitous as it was, the flood provided a break from routine; in some cases the tension of the emergency was welcome relief from the dull and repetitive life of the rural South, especially for young people. Rescue workers, enjoying the challenge of the river, invariably vowed that they would gladly volunteer again, for the rescue work was personally rewarding. In one way, then, the disaster was terrible—yet people remember not only the terror, but also more lighthearted moments.

Catastrophic as the flood was, the death toll would have grown into the thousands had not the Red Cross and its affiliated agencies rushed in to rescue people and care for them in their distress. Secretary of Commerce Herbert Hoover coordinated this gigantic effort; at times he commanded an army of 33,000 in the relief effort. Only 1400 of these were paid workers; over 31,000 people volunteered to save and care for their brothers and sisters. Perhaps most memorable to those involved was the fact that during the emergency people rose above the restricting customs of race and caste; the first concern was to rescue the perishing, then to aid and comfort them in their distress, and finally to shepherd them back home. Of course there were irregularities, exploitation, peonage, pilfering, sexual problems, and other abuses. Yet with a cast of a million, the drama was acted out with few flawed lines.

2

crevasse

In the vernacular of the people who live along the Mississippi River, a *crevasse* is a break in the levee. That single word carried dread, often panic, for water twenty feet above the land level bursts out across the fields, sweeping all before it. The April 21 crevasse at Mound Landing, Mississippi, about eighteen miles north of Greenville, sent shock waves through the entire area.

When the levee broke early in the morning, men were frantically tossing sandbags on top of it, trying to keep the river harnessed. Many workers were killed when it collapsed; no one will ever know how many. At first the press reported hundreds, but later the figures were reduced; no accurate count could be made, for the confusion was too great. Charlie Williams of Greenville was there directing the high-water fight; he said that the levee "just seemed to move forward as if 100 feet of it was *pushed out* by the river." At that very moment General Alexander G. Paxton was in Greenville, talking on the phone to the levee workers at Mound Landing. " 'We can't hold it much longer,' " the general recalled hearing. "Then followed three words that I shall remember as long as I live—'There she goes.' "[1]

It was as if the flood had struck last week instead of nearly fifty years ago. Cora Lee Campbell sat on her front porch in Greenville, some eighteen miles south of

A typical scene along a levee as men filled sandbags to prevent the river from overtopping the levee. This photograph was taken near White Castle, Louisiana. (Ed Supple)

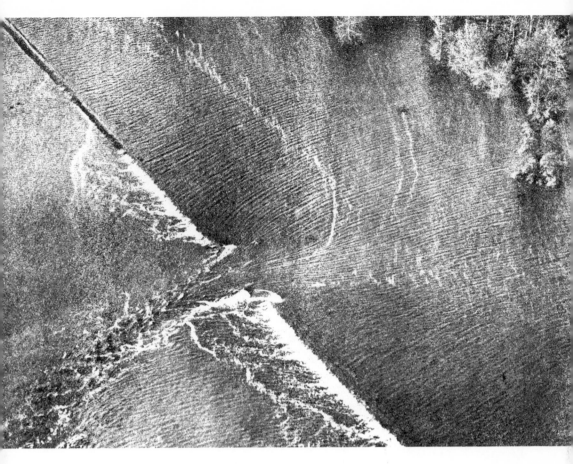

Scott, where she had lived in 1927. "They was working on that levee, and it was real pitiful, and they were working on it with them there sacks, trying to daub 'em and everything. It was on, I think, Thursday morning that I got up, and I walked across that long bridge, and I just did make it back across. See, the Lord just was with me. A lady sent for me to come, Miss Anne, to come over to her home; she had something for me. That was in Scott, over in Scott. I runned over there; by the time I got across that long bridge, that bridge done this-away, parted, right in the middle.

"And so I run and run and run, and when I got home the bells was ringing, the whistles was blowing, and, oh, it was a terrible time. I picked this boy, Roosevelt Campbell, Jr., up on my hip to run, and his teeth was agoing br-br-br-br, thataway, you know, and made it to

The Mound Landing, Mississippi, crevasse was one of the worst. A large section of the levee collapsed, sweeping workers atop it away and giving refugees little time to flee. (*The Flood of 1927*)

15

Temporary shelters on the levee at Greenville. The "little bitty little houses" that Cora Lee Campbell described must have been similar to these. (Mississippi Levee Commissioners, G. Ramsey Russell Collection)

the levee. And when we made it to the levee, chile, them there bubbles was just boiling, boiling, boiling, boiling. That water was deep'n as it come.

"We stayed on the levee three nights and two days, and we didn't have nowhere to lay down. There was a lot of folks on the levee, my father and this child Roosevelt Campbell, my husband, his father, and all the rest of the other people around us. We made little bitty little houses, just big enough for a child to get in, and I laid down there on a army blanket that I raised this child in and the water just come up on me, and I had to take him and lay him in my breast to keep him dry, from getting chilled. It didn't do me no good. Then, in three days a boat come and it took us to Rosedale, and the boat it like to sunk, oh Lord, it was a time. The boat like to sunk, they was so many peoples on the boat, and then they was some people was so ill and mean till they didn't want to get on the boat."[2]

T. H. "Buck" Pryor of Jonesboro, Arkansas, was on the boat that picked up the refugees at Scott. His recollection, written to Mississippi Educational Television after seeing a recent special program on the flood, adds a significant footnote to the rescue of the Scott refugees. "We went up river and docked at the break at Scott, Miss. There were about 300 people on the Levee. Dr. Douglas [S. W. Douglas] and I were on the upper deck when the Captain lowered the gangplank and we saw him walk up the gangplank to be met by two big men, each with a gun on his hip. We could not hear the conversation but we saw the Captain dejectedly turn and come back to the ship.

"Dr. Douglas picked up his Black Bag and said, 'Follow me'—I did. The Captain told Dr. Douglas that the two big men with guns said that they were not going to let us take those people off the Levee.

"Dr. Douglas brushed the Captain aside, strode up the gangplank and he was then met by these two men with guns on hips. I was right behind him—and *scared*.

"The doctor said—and I hope I can repeat verbatim but it's been a long time ago and you will please excuse the language but am trying to repeat Dr. Douglas—*verbatim*—I think he said—'Apparently you two gentlemanly sons-of-bitches are in charge here and you have told the Captain that we are not going to be permitted to minister to these people—now I come here by authority of American Red Cross and the God of all creation—if either of you has guts enough to pull the gun you carry please start now or get out of my way and I don't believe either of you has the guts';—those two gun-carrying Mississippi fellows stood aside—we went on the Levee—we found the sick and infirm—we loaded all on the Barges and left those two 'gun-carrying' fellows there all alone."[3]

After the river broke out at Mound Landing, it spread across the Mississippi Delta. The water did not race across the land as one pictures a flood gushing through a mountain valley (the Johnstown flood often comes to mind); rather, it moved at a pace of some fourteen miles a day. Everyone who saw the water and heard it had that image branded in their minds forever, for it had the eeriness of a full eclipse of the sun, unsettling, chilling.

Whether in Mississippi or in other flooded areas, the description varied little. Louise Cowan of Greenville, who kept a journal during the flood, wrote down a planter's impression of the approaching water. "Standing on the veranda of his handsome home he saw the

A boatload of refugees headed to Vicksburg on April 28, several days after Cora Lee Campbell escaped from Scott aboard a similar boat. (Gordon Cotton)

Barely showing the name, Issaquena, Mississippi. (Mississippi State Archives)

The flood kept the plantation bell silent for several months. Men, women, and mules fled to the high ground. "A tossing, seething yellow sea as far as the eye can reach in every direction this morning," wrote Fred Chaney from Metcalfe, Mississippi, on April 22. "Houses and familiar objects look grotesque and strange indeed —cut in two by the climbing oblivion of the water line." (Mississippi State Archives)

flood approach in the form of a tan colored wall seven feet high, and with a roar as of a mighty wind." East of Greenville in Leland, Edwin Bagley, who was fourteen years old in 1927, recalled the water rolling to Deer Creek, pouring over the bank into the creek, filling it, and creeping onward. "Talk about a distressing sound," he said, "people screaming, dogs barking, and the sound of that water, like a stream of water in a mountain."[4]

The sometimes whispering, sometimes roaring sound of the water flowing across the land left its mark on the memories of people as well as on the land. (Boots Walker)

At Metcalfe, only four miles out of Greenville, Fred Chaney was already in a boxcar, his home for the duration of the flood. "At nine o'clock we could hear the rustle of waters in the woods a mile North of our box car haven," he wrote in his reminiscences of the flood. "It sounded not unlike the rising rush of the first gust of wind before an oncoming storm and a shiver shot up and down my spine as the rustling noise grew louder and its true significance plumbed the depths of my mind. Before I reached the railroad track the water was swirling around my feet! From somewhere out of the night rose the piercing wail of a negro woman's hysterical scream."[5]

In Greenville, General Paxton remembered April 21 vividly. "It was about as wild a day as I have experienced in all my life," and that included three wars. "I have never seen anything equal to it. The fire whistle was blowing repeatedly and people were swarming down the streets in throngs. Pandemonium broke out everywhere." Across the river in Arkansas City, Grady F. Jones reported a similar experience. "All the cattle was lowing, all the dogs barking, every rooster crowing, babies crying, women screaming and all hurrying to the high places."[6]

Greenville residents knew the flood was on its way, but they hoped that the protection levee around the town would keep the water out. At the same time they feared another break in the main levee along the river. It was the tension of not knowing if the protection levee or the main levee would hold, not knowing exactly how or at what time the water would reach town, that made the night of April 21 so tense in Greenville.

"We sat up that night until after midnight in terror and as the wind got worse we decided the levee would

THE COMMERCIAL APPEAL.

VOL. CXII—NO. 112   MEMPHIS, TENN., FRIDAY MORNING, APRIL 22, 1927—TWENTY-SIX PAGES

GREENVILLE FLOODED; PEOPLE FLEE FOR LIVES; LEVEES SNAP UNDER STRAIN LEAVING PATH OF DEATH AND DESTRUCTION IN WAKE OF WORST FLOO[

have to go and we had better get to a stronger building," wrote Mrs. E. G. Gilbert a few weeks later. "So we all dressed and tied up quilts and sandwiches. My husband ran up town in a car to see if he could learn how the levee was holding. Before he got back the whistle blew.

"Of course, every one thought it was the main levee. I had picked up my baby in a blanket and we ran the two blocks. The wind was cold and cut off our breaths. We were frantic, expecting water to engulf us any minute.

"I felt so sorry for the children, but I was out of breath and could not talk to them even after we had reached the courthouse safely. They were shaking with terror. We were almost the first to get to the courthouse, but in a little while there were 1,000 people there."[7]

The flood water quickly topped the protection levee and entered Greenville on April 22 before daylight. Louise Henry Cowan stayed in her home and at daybreak watched the water slowly edge along the gutters. "Slowly, oh, so slowly, the silver line widened, and then there was a silver thread in our gutter also. They approached each other until they touched the raised and green car track in the center of the street. At six o'clock Washington Avenue was a sheet of shallow, muddy water. It was no longer a thing of beauty."[8]

William Cobb, Robert Murphy, and Jesse L. Gray were standing in a churchyard after Sunday services when they recalled the crevasse at Pendleton, Arkansas, just a few miles across the flat fields on the Arkansas River. The levee had given way at Pendleton a few hours after the break at Mound Landing.

"On that night that the levee broke," began William Cobb, "my daddy went out and he could see the water coming across the field. Our house was about, I guess, eighteen inches off the ground, and he come back in the house and he say, I see the water coming across the field there. It had done filled up a big slough between our house and the levee, and it had got level out there. So he come back in the house and stayed about twenty minutes, went back out there and said, the water done made it up here to the house and it's running across the bottom step. The house had three steps, coming up in to the porch. Then he went on back into the house and then in about twenty minutes more the water had done got up to the top step. And about ten o'clock that night we were moving a few bed things up in the loft part of

Only levee tops, telephone poles, housetops, Indian mounds, and trees protruded above the flood. (Red Cross)

William Cobb and Robert Murphy lived very close to the crevasse at Pendleton, Arkansas. (Arkansas History Commission)

In the center of the picture is a blue hole. The water rushing through the crevasse dredges out a hole, sometimes a hundred feet deep. The effect of the current can be seen in the lower part of the photograph. (Arkansas History Commission)

the house. And there's where we was until the next morning, and we stayed up there two nights and three days. Finally a seaplane come along. My daddy had done cut a hole where he could look out on the outside, and he was waving a white rag when that seaplane come by. And in about two hours after then, it was, a gas boat pulled up there and taken us all to the levee. We lived up there on the levee until the water went down."[9]

Robert Murphy lived in the same neighborhood as William Cobb in 1927, and he also described the flood, often comparing it with his neighbor's account. "We was living somewhere right in yonder, about where you see that tall house, just over behind them trees a little bit. Just like he said, the levee broke about, um, six thirty or seven o'clock, somewhere along like that. And it was a airplane, when it broke they had men out there working, well, when it broke that airplane just circled all around here. We had the boat tied at the front gate. Well, I guess about eight o'clock daddy told me to go out there and bring the boat and tie it to the porch.

22

Well, when I went out I was intending to pull it on the ground, but when I went out, I stepped in the water, and I said, uh, uh, daddy. That water was, look like to me, that water was over my head; wasn't hardly up to my knees. But it had covered everything and just like he said, about then it was right at the bottom step. Well, in about, I don't know, a half hour, no longer than an hour, it had come on up. Well, as he said, we already had a whole lot of our stuff already up in the loft because we had carried all the mules out to high ground, and all the family was gone but me and my daddy and my brother. We were still there. During the time while we was there, we made a scaffold and put the hogs up in the barn; and the chickens, we scaffolded them up in the hen house, you know, kind of up high, while we was up in the loft. We had it so we could go up and come down, but we was up in the loft. During that flood, we lost one hen; it flew off and flew out in that water and drowned. But we didn't lose none of the hogs; we had about twelve or fifteen head of hogs. . . . So after that we stayed there, oh, till up in the next day, and then we went out to where my mother and sisters was, then out there on high ground. We could come backwards and forwards and feed those hogs up in the loft, and the chickens. The water got about four foot in the house, but it didn't hurt a thing. . . . The reason it

Near Holland Landing, Mississippi, these families were trying to save their cows and pigs on this improvised raft. (Gordon Cotton)

Frank Cashman reported
in the Vicksburg *Evening
Post* that flying over the
flooded towns reminded
him of "little Venices," but
"they are deserted."
(Hoover Library)

didn't, it was woods all around there where the water wasn't swift, and it just come slowly through them woods. . . . And you could hear it roaring a long ways off. Kind of like, they say, a tornado. Near about that loud."[10]

Jesse L. Gray lived up the river in Jefferson County. There it "was not quite as severe," he remembered, though "it was pretty deep. And we moved to higher ground, out to Gray Keys gin. We stayed out there about three weeks, out there at the gin fore we could move back home. But the water did get up waist high in the house where we lived. Whole lots of families was at this gin and cooked and ate out there, had an open fire and cooked and ate and all on cotton seed, with what few things we brought, till we got a chance to go back."[11]

William Cobb said that life was pretty good on the levee where he stayed, for that time of year. Some of the people left, he recalled. "The boat come and taken them to Mississippi, off the levee. They said they fared pretty good, over there. They didn't fare too good getting back. Some of them didn't even get back. I know one man they separated him and his wife. He stayed here and his wife went over there. She stayed over there, didn't come back."[12]

26

Six days after the levee broke at Pendleton, Arkansas, Governor John E. Martineau received a warning that "the village of Watson is virtually wiped out. How the farmers, both white and black, saved themselves in the back country, I do not know."

Watson was then and is now an east Arkansas village of some 350 people, located a few miles south of the Arkansas River. When the levee broke several miles away at Pendleton on April 21, the flood waters rushed in. Watson native C. D. Dupree was fifteen years old in 1927; today he is the mayor. Watson was covered by the flood waters, Dupree admits, but it was not wiped out. Most inhabitants went immediately to the levee, where boats picked them up and carried them to refugee camps in Mississippi. Dupree stayed behind. "The water got too high and we'd done waited too late then to leave out of here, couldn't get anywhere, so we went to the second story of the hotel. And there was numerous people who lived in the second story of the school house auditorium. And quite a few people lived on top of buildings, had tents; see that flat top building yonder?" he asked as he pointed out the window. "They had tents on top of that."

Dupree was sitting in a booth in his bar, Monk's Place, on May 23, 1975, some forty-eight years after the flood. As he spoke, he opened his family album and began showing old photographs of Watson, before, during, and after the 1927 flood.

Things were boring during the high water; people who stayed in the second story of the hotel "just played cards. They all kind of cooked together and eat together. Same way as the people that stayed on top of the school house and on the second story." The refugees were sitting out what was usually one of the most active seasons of farming and business. "There wasn't any crops made that year at all here. Course I was at the age where it didn't worry me; I didn't realize what it was, really," he admitted. He continued turning through the album, explaining the pictures of the flood.[13]

The C. D. Dupree Family Album Watson, Arkansas

"That was Red Fork Levee, about four miles north of here. It's about three miles below where the levee broke, down river." As Eric Hardy of Monticello, Arkansas, remembered it, "They had hundreds of men down there and laborers and plenty of help, but they just didn't have enough help to cope with that Arkansas River. It was just a little bit more than men could do." (C. D. Dupree)

"That's my grandfather, D. E. Dobson. That water was just coming up. It hadn't got high enough to get into the building. It was about a week before it reached its peak here." (C. D. Dupree)

"They're bringing timber out to the railroad, loading it on cars, taking it out 'fore the flood got hold of it. That's F. A. Newlin. This was when the water was first rising." (C. D. Dupree)

28

"Those cars are on top of the railroad platform. Those cars went on under. That platform set right next to the railroad, right out there." (C. D. Dupree)

The J. R. Ferguson Hotel in Watson, where C. D. Dupree and his family waited out the flood. (C. D. Dupree)

"This is my home. It's remodeled now, but it still has the same kind of roof." (C. D. Dupree)

The levee at Arkansas City served as a refugee camp. Other refugees lived in the upper stories of buildings. (Arkansas History Commission)

ARKANSAS CITY SUFFERS FLOOD BY BACK WATER

Is Inundated as Result Of Break in Pendleton Levee

DEATH LIST GROWING

Unconfirmed Figures Place Toll for Arkansas at 87.

MOST STREAMS FALLING

Arkansas City is just opposite Mound Landing, and when the levee gave way across the river the people in Arksansas sighed with relief. Yet when the crevasse came at Pendleton later the same day, the water rushed toward Arkansas City, and on Sunday morning it was approaching the town from the rear. "I was in Sunday School," Verna Reitzammer remembers (she was eighteen at the time), "and my Sunday School teacher said, 'Let's drive out,' and that was about eleven o'clock. She said, 'Let's drive out and see where the water is.' Someone said it was coming in this way, so we got in her car and drove out the highway and at the first bridge before you get to Boggy Bayou the water was creeping on the highway. We were afraid to go to Boggys to turn around, so we turned around in the middle of the road, and came back to town. To me, to those who saw it coming over the ridge, it was rolling, but to me it was moving sorta fast but slow, too.

"It wasn't just rolling in and lapping like some of these breaks you have on the dams where it just sweeps everybody in. Well, this wasn't that way. In fact, it was coming in slow enough that I went home and ate dinner, and we had this little store down here in the western part of town. My dad sent me down there to put the stuff up on the counters; he'd had a stroke and was helpless. So I was down there working, took a girl friend of mine down there. I was just putting stuff up on the counter and looked, and the water was coming in the door. And so Margie said, 'Well, I'm going to get home while I can.' So she left and had to wade out to get home, but I stayed down there thinking, well, the water won't rise *that* much. When it did start really coming in the door, well, I called my mother and told her that it was up too high then for me to wade out, so she tried to find somebody to come get me out from down there. There was a meat block out down there. The store was up about, took two steps to get up there, I'd say about three feet high off the ground. Anyway, there was a meat block out there, and I went out there and sat on the meat block, and a boat was coming down the street. So then I hailed Mr. Shelton, asked if he wouldn't give me a lift to the levee. I crawled in his boat and came on. We didn't come clear to the levee but down here to where there was dry land. I was able to get out of the boat and still walk home on these two streets. So the water came from that western direction coming into town, but how fast it came in then, I just don't remember because it just gradually came."[14]

Her husband, Rocky, was also in the grocery business; his store, with the residence upstairs, was on the street facing the levee, just where it is today. "I was working down at the store putting the stuff on one shelf,

The first of the flood water entering Arkansas City. Later the flood reached to the point of the arrow on the right. *(The Flood of 1927)*

31

you know, and I'd say, well, I can go to sleep an hour and get up and go down there again and the water was about to catch it there, so I'd put it up another shelf. Then it got so deep in there that it floated the counters out; the counters were floating and I floated them out there and tied them to the post so I could get 'em later on."[15]

When the water did begin to creep into buildings, the people tried to get all their furniture upstairs, but some of it was too heavy. "I remember," Verna Reitzammer said, "sitting up on the upstairs steps and watching my piano floating out the front door, piece by piece, one key right after the other. That's the only thing I cried about in the flood."[16]

The current left holes behind that resembled bomb craters. This photo was taken south of Little Rock, Arkansas, on May 10, as the flood receded. (Arkansas History Commission)

Though the Reitzammers and even William Cobb, Robert Murphy, and Jesse L. Gray seem to have taken the flood in stride, voicing little terror at their misfortunes, other refugees were less fortunate. When the levees broke along the Arkansas River in Jefferson County, hundreds of people, mostly tenant farmers, had no refuge—no upstairs, no cotton gin—to flee to; they headed toward Pine Bluff with the water lapping at their heels. Some from the north bank of the Arkansas River made it as far as the Free Bridge, a large steel structure that spanned the river, but because the approaches to the bridge were lower than the main span the people were stranded there, unable to go back or forward. The weather was miserable, cold and rainy, and since the water was too rough for boats to rescue them, they huddled on that steel island for several days. Jesse L. Gray had heard stories from the people out there, he said. The water was right under the bridge, and Gray took his hands and put one on top of the other and began to slap them together—slap, slap, slap. "The water would do that," he said, "up on the bottom of the bridge."[17]

Lula Toler, a home demonstration agent from Pine Bluff, gave up her usual duties when the flood struck and became a full-time relief worker. Her report on activities during the first stages of the flood explains the dilemma on the Free Bridge. "My first days work with the sufferers were ones long to be remembered. The scene was most pitiful and shall ever haunt me while life lasts. The screams of the people and the lowing of cattle could be heard in the distance. At least five hundred from the lower-lands made their escape to the Arkansas River bridge which is said to be one mile in length and well constructed. Here they were marooned for three days and nights. Our only means to get them to safety was by row boats. The first day the wind was so high, causing the waves to be so rough that no one dared to venture near until night, when one Mr. Fitzpatrick made one trip landing twenty, but came very near losing his life.

"Night came with a terrible storm and we were forced to leave the post of watch, leaving the refugees looking

Bridges often served as islands of safety. This bridge across the Sunflower River at Holland Landing, Mississippi, harbored 700 refugees until they could be rescued. (Gordon Cotton)

The Holland Landing bridge after the refugees had been removed. To the left are hogs and dogs running across the driftwood. When the dogs got hungry, they killed and ate the hogs, but when the water rose higher and the driftwood broke up, the dogs drowned. In other areas of refuge, where there was enough food, animals managed to reach a temporary truce until the waters fell. (Gordon Cotton)

up to God, who doeth all things well, while the angry waters rolled on. Women, with babies in their arms, men and women, bent with years, waited on the bridge casting wistful eyes to the land of safety, hungry, wet, and tired through the long hours of the stormy night, listening to the dashing of the angry waves, watching the drowning of the cattle and the floating of their belongings.

"While it was yet dark, we made our way back to the spot where we had prepared comfort for our refugees. The wind ceased and the boat was soon on its journey making a trip every hour and a half, landing 35 at a time. We learned that two babies had been born on the bridge."[18]

Despite the disruption in the hinterland, life in Pine Bluff, at least in the higher parts of the city, was fairly normal. Lucyle Cantley was in the antique and book business in 1927, as she is now, and remembers that the

Main Street in Pine Bluff, Arkansas. Life went on half under water and half above. (Louise N. Doak)

tone in the community was serious. Since only part of the city had been flooded, life went on half under water and half above. "The old depot at State and Fourth was where you caught your boat. Sometimes you got in a skiff, hand propelled, and then you caught a faster boat when you got to the depot, you know. It was uncanny to hear somebody say, 'Oh, I've got to run; I've got to catch my boat to work, or I got to catch by boat home, or whatever.'" She also remembered that the flood floated several pieces of furniture her way.[19]

The Arkansas River broke levees and flooded land from far west of Little Rock to the mouth of the river, north of Arkansas City. Naturally, people farther south became more and more apprehensive. New crevasses seemed sure, and apprehension centered upon where the new breaks would come and how high the water would rise.

The water that rushed down through the Mississippi Delta from the Mound Landing crevasse skirted the hills to the east, ran through the Yazoo River basin, and eventually entered the main stream again near Vicksburg. E. C. Woodyear lives opposite Vicksburg, at Mound, Louisiana, near where he lived in 1927. "My job during the high water crisis was patrolling the levee at night," he explained. "Practically all of the work during that time was accomplished with mule and man power. We did not have the machinery that we have now. The reason that we were in such a bad location here was due to a crevasse north of us at Mound Land-

East 6th Street in Pine Bluff. As Lucyle Cantley remembered, it was uncanny to hear somebody say, "Oh, I've got to run; I've got to catch my boat to work, or I got to catch my boat home, or whatever." (Louise N. Doak)

This remarkable series of aerial photographs shows the widening of the Cabin Teele crevasse. The photographs proved invaluable to the U.S. Corps of Engineers in studying flood control.

The crevasse at Cabin Teele, Louisiana, May 3, 1927, 5:30 p.m. At that time it was 150 feet wide. (Corps of Engineers, Vicksburg, 67-AM-189)

ing which relieved the pressure from that point south until the water came back into the Yazoo River at Vicksburg. There just wasn't any way that we could hold all of that water. About ten or twelve miles north of here, they had relief, but from here on down it just hit us right in the face. This caused the Cabin Teele crevasse on the west side of the river. There just wasn't any way that it could be held. It just had to go.

"We had a humorous story about what happened when the big plantation bell was rung by mistake, warning everyone that the levee had broken. It had been prearranged with all of the people living on the plantation and all within hearing distance that the bell would not be rung unless the levee broke. Due to a false alarm, they rang the bell. Everyone hurried to the levee which was the only high ground that we had. There was a man working on the levee, who had his trunk packed with his best possessions. When he heard the bell, he ran home, picked up the trunk and ran to the levee with it. When he found that it was a false alarm, he was going to carry his trunk back, but he couldn't pick it up. So they told the story that two of them tried to pick it up and carry it and they couldn't. They had to get a mule and slide to haul the trunk back to his house."

The Cabin Teele crevasse, May 3, at 5:50 p.m. (Corps of Engineers, Vicksburg, 67-AM-184)

The Cabin Teele crevasse
the day after the break.
(Corps of Engineers, Vicksburg, 67-AM-182)

The water continued to rise, and Woodyear joined in the high water fight topping off the levee. "We had to go in there and build it up with sacks. We stacked them up, and there were a lot of sacks in some places. Up there where it broke you could stand on the top knot of the sacks, and you couldn't see over the sacks. You can imagine how high it was built up. I was close by when it broke. Everyone knew it was coming and was pretty well packed up and ready to get to high ground. A lot of people went to Vicksburg. You could hear the steamboats coming down the river at night with boatloads of people on them. There was boatload after boatload of refugees going to Vicksburg. Vicksburg was headquarters for the Red Cross during the flood. They came in and looked after the refugees during the flood and helped rehabilitate them after the flood. They did a wonderful job.

"I lived on Sparta Plantation, two miles from where the Cabin Teele crevasse occurred at one o'clock in the afternoon of May 3, 1927. The water began to back up and started coming in that night. The Mound Landing crevasse caused much more destruction and damage than the Cabin Teele crevasse. The Cabin Teele crevasse broke slowly and did not blow out all at once like the Mound Landing crevasse did.

The Cabin Teele crevasse, May 8, at 9:15 a.m. This was five days after the break. (Corps of Engineers, Vicksburg, 67-AM-183)

Driving mules through McGehee to higher ground. (Desha Public Library)

"Most of the old house sites were on high ground and never went under. They had been built by old timers who knew where the high spots were located."

On the night of the break he helped drive cattle to the levee and remembers that he had never seen the mosquitoes so bad. He spent the night in a car on the levee. The next day boats pushed barges over to the levee from Vicksburg, and the cattle were loaded and taken there. Later most of the stock died, the mules from anthrax and the hogs from cholera; few of the horses died, Woodyear remembers.[20]

By mid-May the Mississippi flood had pushed into bayou country south of the Red River. Stretching south of Red River runs the Bayou des Glaises, a stream heavily leveed to protect Marksville, Cottonport, Moreauville, Simmesport, Plaucheville, and a number of small towns in the sugar-growing area of Avoyelles Parish. Like E. C. Woodyear, the people along the Bayou des Glaises knew that the levees would fail and that a flood would immerse them.

In June 1975 Tucker Couvillon, nineteen years old in 1927, recalled that he knew the levees were about to collapse. "I knew the situation was bad," he said in his Cajun accent. "They were expecting a crevasse some-

where; we didn't know where." Being young and interested in excitement, Couvillon started out from Marksville looking for one. "The first crevasse happened
between Long Bridge and Cottonport. I was in Cottonport and I got caught. Then I had to walk back. I
didn't have the slightest idea what a crevasse was. I
didn't know how much water came through a crevasse."
Thus he innocently walked through a roaring crevasse
to get home, along a road that was already flooding
when he started, and it got worse. "A barbed wire fence
is not the nicest thing," he explained. "When I was walking across that road, I got scratched up going and coming. And that was just the beginning." When I asked
him if he was confident he would make it through the
crevasse that roared some four hundred yards from the
road he was walking along, he replied, "I had my
doubts, I had my doubts.

"I was young and strong and eager, and I love excitement, but still when you are confronted with problems
like I was," he paused. "I was thinking of my mother;
boy, she is going to wring me—if I get back. When I
first started it was knee deep, and when I ended up it
was waist deep. I walked, I'd say, three miles. I had no
more business there than the man in the moon. It was
just that I wanted a little bit of excitement, and I got it
too. But I got a little too much."[21]

The Cottonport crevasse was only the beginning, for
the entire network of Bayou des Glaises levees crumbled. Major breaks occurred at Kleinwood, Bordelonville, Willard Station, Moreauville, and Hamburg, and
there were minor ones in other places. It took the flood
waters only two days to destroy the entire Bayou des
Glaises levee system.

On May 17 the levee along the Atchafalaya River
broke at Melville—a disastrous surprise, for it was
thought to be a strong levee. Turner Catledge, then a
reporter for the Memphis *Commercial Appeal*, who
often traveled with relief director Herbert Hoover, happened to be near Melville when the levee collapsed.
"The water ripped out a hole about 2,000 feet wide. It
was one of the highest and considered one of the best
levees along the whole river. The break was on the west

Unidentified levee worker
in Louisiana. (Louisiana
Dept. of Public Works)

Mississippi River gauge at
Plaquemine Locks. The
reading is 42.5 feet. The
Mississippi River rose to 43
feet at Plaquemine and
remained above 42.5 feet
for a week in mid-May.
(Iberville Parish Library,
Mrs. Philip J. Neubig Collection)

Levee work near Geismar,
Louisiana, where a cre-
vasse occurred May 18,
1927. (Louisiana Dept. of
Public Works)

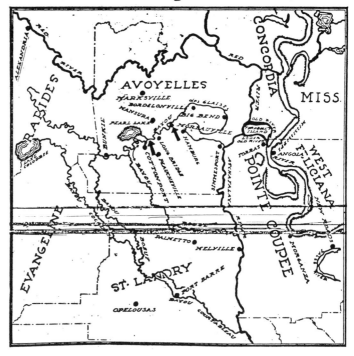

Flood Breaks Through Des Glaises Levee

side, about 200 yards south of the Texas & Pacific Railroad bridge across the Atchafalaya.

"The water leaped through the crevasse with such fury that it spread in three distinct currents. One force shot straight west, wrecking houses, barns and fences as it went. Another shot back due north, quickly eating out 50-foot sections of the Texas & Pacific Railroad dump, thus allowing the water to go up into the town proper and completely inundate it. The break through the railway embankment looked like a river crevasse within itself. Breakers were shooting through and leaping over each other way up into the streets of the town.

"A third current struck out from the south. It swept everything before it. Washtubs, work benches, house-

The current near Moreauville, Louisiana. (Paul Coco)

An aerial view of the crevasse at Melville, Louisiana, on the Atchalafaya River. The bridge tender perished when the span of the railroad bridge fell into the river. (National Archives, U.S. Army Air Force, 18-AN-5873)

hold furniture, chickens and domestic animals were floating away with one of the three currents.

"The Atchafalaya River is one of the most tricky and certainly now one of the fiercest streams in the whole country. It is hitting at the runway on the Texas & Pacific bridge at Melville in fierce torrents and rapids, compared by members of the Hoover party to the rapids in the vicinity of Niagara Falls. The water literally dives under the bridge, rolls one breaker on another as it comes from under the structure, roaring to such a degree that it drowns out the rumbling of trains across it. However, no regular trains will cross that bridge now for some time, as the new break this morning cut the line at Melville. The next day one span of the railroad bridge collapsed into the river, killing the bridge tender."[22]

One week later another major levee broke along the Atchalafaya River, at McCrea, Louisiana. It became obvious that the entire bayou country in southern Louisiana would be flooded, though many residents stubbornly doubted the predictions. Tradition has it that many Cajuns refused to believe the water was coming into town, even though they could see the first trickles in the gutters. One woman reportedly continued to hang out her wash even as she watched the flood come down the street toward her.[23]

Six miles east of New Iberia, Louisiana, Mrs. W. I. Spencer wrote from the Morbihan plantation on May 26, 1927, about what happened there when the flood approached. "Everything became tense. The gay songs of the negroes trailed away into ominous silence; groups gathering here and there, hurriedly leaving for their different cabins to spread the news and to get ready. Some still were doubtful and started out to investigate for themselves, soon returning though with a wild look on their faces. There were hurried preparations made to leave—the water all the time silently yet, creeping farther and farther under their houses, up their steps—this from the Bayou—it was coming from the bayou north of the plantation too, but the big wave came rolling from seemingly nowhere, spreading over the whole hillside and coming over in ditches, furrows, low places, silently yet, but rushing as if being chased by some great monster.

"Then came a murmuring, a distant roaring—everyone seemed to sense danger then and prepared to get on the highest ground and the tallest buildings. By this time water was rushing and roaring in all ditches and

Levee workers watch the Atchalafaya River eat into the bank at McCrea, Louisiana. Later the levee gave way. *(The Flood of 1927)*

Along the Jefferson Highway in Melville. Turner Catledge wrote that "Breakers were shooting through and leaping over each other way up into the streets of the town." (Louisiana Dept. of Public Works)

drains over most of the hillside to the Bayou. Above all you could hear children's cries, women's screams, and petitions to 'de good Lawd' to save them. All families had left their homes by now and the highest place on the plantation was full of darkies, bedding, dogs, chicken coops—everything they thought of bringing in their mad flight.

"The waters seemed to lull for a bit, then fires sprang up on the high place and the men were cooking the noon meal while waiting for the boats to come and get them. But their food wasn't cooked before the waters seemed to gather force, gain in rapidity of motion, and loudness. Great masses of dirty foam began forming where there was the least resistance only to be broken loose by the rising of swiftly growing currents."[24]

It must have been at about the same time that young A. Lewis Bernard and his parents started out from New Iberia on the St. Martinville road and reached the Missouri Pacific roundhouse. "And there was a grade crossing, where the railroad track is built up high," he said, "and it was like a levee. And the water was beginning to pour over the top of the railroad tracks from the north into the town of New Iberia. Bayou Teche at New Iberia was not flooded. This was one of the things that Dad proclaimed in advance would happen and everybody thought he was crazy. They said the only way that New Iberia can flood is if the bayou rises, and he said no, it will not come from the bayou, it will come from the lowlands from the Spanish Lake area. And this is exactly what happened. The water came down through that great trough of which Spanish Lake is the end, and it came and it hit this embankment where the railroad was and started spilling over. And it was right then and there standing on that railroad track with his Kodak in his hand, that Dad said, 'Momma, you and Lewis are going to leave as quick as we can get you on the train tomorrow or the next day at the latest.' He said, 'I want you out of here; this town is going under.' So I guess it was two days later that we actually left. By the time we did leave, our back yard was flooded. The back yard was toward Bayou Teche from Main Street. So we left, and of course Dad was busy with his Kodak taking pictures."[25]

44

In 1927 Myrtle Turner Staples was a junior in high school in New Iberia. Like most young people caught up in the flood, she admits that she was afraid her mind "was on having fun and not thinking (as I should have been) of all the destruction the flood was causing and had caused." She first learned that there was a flood danger when her cousin, A. L. LeMaire, Sr., told her that boys were being taken out of school to work on the levees. The part they worked on held, but the levee gave way on the Atchafalaya River at Henderson, and the water entered New Iberia from St. Martinville by what was then Lallande's Store.

Unlike her friends, Myrtle Turner carried along a camera, explaining that "since my father, L. M. Turner, was a professional photographer before I was born, photography runs in my family, and I suppose that it was just second nature to have a camera in my hands wherever I went.

"When I think back over those days I think of the risks we took as we walked barefooted in this high water to the Shadows on the Teche and the ride down the Bayou in those little boats, the high water and the snakes which we later saw all over town, some right in our own front yard, right up to the bottom step. And how the frogs serenaded us all night as long as the high water lasted. But as teen-agers, I suppose all we could think of was fun."[26]

Myrtle Turner Staples's Album New Iberia, Louisiana

Photo taken by I. A. Martin in front of the Albert Estorge home, now torn down and replaced by a modern Post Office. Myrtle Turner Staples explained the photograph. "The 'carriage' is really a milk wagon driven by one of my uncles, Mr. A. A. LeMaire, who was a dairyman and delivered the milk around town. He is being assisted by one of his sons, Maurice Turner LeMaire, and Lucius Stredit." (Carroll Studio)

Mrs. Gladys Calhoon Case and her daughter, Patsy, now Mrs. W. J. Stansbury, on East Main Street, looking toward East End away from the business district. (Myrtle Turner Staples)

Near Lallande's Store, where the water came in from St. Martin-ville on Jane Street. (Myrtle Turner Staples)

46

"The Convent was known as Mount Carmel Convent then, but is now known as the Catholic Girl's High School. It is situated right across from the Bridge Keeper's home on Duperier Avenue. This is across the Bayou Teche near the heart of the business district where the bridge was destroyed." (Myrtle Turner Staples)

"The picture of the relatives in the swim suits was taken in the back yard of Mr. Willie Weeks Hall's home on Main Street, 'The Shadows on the Teche.' Mr. Hall asked my Uncle, Mr. M. B. Le-Maire, to bring us all over and he would take us for a ride down Bayou Teche in his boats. In the boat are Mr. Willie Weeks Hall, Katherine Rose, now Mrs. E. C. Wells, Lillie Mae Rose, now Mrs. Gonsoulin, Ruth LeMaire, now Mrs. Vaughn Taylor, and Gladys Calhoon, now Mrs. Gladys Calhoon Case." (Myrtle Turner Staples)

47

The Bridge Keeper's home, across the Bayou Teche to the right of the bridge, and across from Mount Carmel Convent on Duperier Avenue. "Whenever a very large boat came down Bayou Teche and blew its whistle, the Bridge Keeper would open and close the bridge night and day. The Bridge Keeper's house was built much lower on the ground near the Bayou than other homes and the top of the house was almost even with the bridge—this is why it went under so quickly." (Myrtle Turner Staples)

"The picture with the car on the front porch is the home I lived in with my aunt and uncle who raised me—Mr. and Mrs. M. B. Le-Maire on Bank Avenue. Planks were used to drive the car onto the porch. Seated from left to right were Mr. M. B. LeMaire, Mrs. J. S. Turner, standing, Patsy Case, now Mrs. W. J. Stansbury, and Earline LeMaire, now Mrs. Harry Lusk." (Myrtle Turner Staples)

Not all of the crevasses were natural breaks; there were two exceptions. On April 23 a ship, the *Inspector,* accidentally rammed a levee south of New Orleans at the Junior Plantation. When the ship first broke the levee, reporters flocked to the scene to discover exactly how serious it was. George W. Healy, Jr., was one of the reporters assigned to the story. In 1962 Healy wrote an article recounting that assignment. "My first connection with the major flood was as a boatman-reporter. When word reached the *Times-Picayune* of the Junior Plantation crevasse, three reporters were assigned to get to the scene. The late Ken Knobloch was assigned to try to make it by automobile on the east bank of the river. Another reporter was told to go down the west bank. I was told to charter a motorboat and go down the middle of the river at night.

"The tough part of that assignment was getting to Junior Plantation without getting shot. Guards armed with shotguns and rifles patrolled every foot of the levee. They patrolled both banks, and any boat or other object coming too close to either bank got, at best, a warning blast.

"After getting shot at, or at least warned several times, we steered the last 20 miles by ear. Lying on deck, under the wheel, I'd put the wheel to the right when there was gunfire on the port side. I knew I was too close to the left bank. When the shots started coming from the starboard side, I'd put the wheel to the left.

The freighter *Inspector* seemed about ready to go into the fields as it poked through the levee at Junior Plantation south of New Orleans. (National Archives, 77-MRF-177)

When it became necessary to dynamite the levee at Caernarvon, south of New Orleans, to save the city from flooding, the "levees only" policy of the Mississippi River Commission and the U.S. Army Corps of Engineers was blown out of existence. *(The Flood of 1927)*

The first day of dynamiting started only a trickle of water through the artificial crevasse. As George W. Healy, Jr., reported, "The first blast, on Friday, April 29, was a flop, literally and figuratively. Soil blown out of the levee went straight up in the air and then flopped down into the holes in the levee's crown whence it had been blown." (Red Cross)

"When I stepped from the motorboat to the levee about 100 feet from the crevasse, I knew I 'had it made'; the first person I saw was Nolan Bruce, engineer in charge of levees in that district and a classmate of mine in college. He not only told me almost everything I needed to know about the crevasse, but he got me to a telephone that was working. Some time later Bill Wiegand of the *Morning Tribune* staff arrived, but the two reporters from the *Times-Picayune* who were trying to travel to the levee break by automobile never got there. I never asked Bill Wiegand how he made it."[27]

The break at Junior Plantation did not lower the river, and New Orleans residents watched anxiously as the water rose up the levee. As the desperate city fathers saw it, the only way to save the city was to make an artificial break in the levee to the south; like pulling the plug in a bathtub, the water would drain out of the river across an improvised spillway. New Orleans merchants promised to care for the people who would be displaced by such a cut in the levee. Again, George Healy reported the action. "Caernarvon, on the east bank of the river between Poydras and Braithwaite, was selected as the site of the levee dynamiting. The first blast, on Friday, April 29, was a flop, literally and figuratively. Soil blown out of the levee went straight up in the air and then flopped down into the holes in the levee's crown whence it had been blown. Twelve hours after the first blast there was only a trickle of water through the Caernarvon openings.

"There was no torrent until 48 hours later, when a diver placed a heavy charge of explosives under the batture in front of the levee. When this charge blew up the batture, the levee collapsed. Hundreds of thousands of cubic feet of water began flowing out of the river every second into a shortcut to Breton Sound. The Carrollton gauge started registering declines in the river stage. New Orleans breathed easier."[28]

If New Orleans breathed easier, so did diver Ted Herbert, who had volunteered to plant the charges under the batture. On May 3 he had entered the water three times, attempting to get the charge in the correct place as the current pushed him to and fro. Once he entered the water "and the terrific current jammed the helmet on his head so hard that he almost strangled before he was dragged back to his skiff."[29]

The crevasse at Caernarvon flooded Plaquemines and St. Bernard parishes, and inhabitants fled to New Orleans, where they were listed among the refugees. With the emergency crevasse, an era of flood control ended; the "levees only" policy had been dynamited out of existence.

But the Mississippi River was not yet finished. In June, as the northern snows melted and more water came south, the river rose and the water oozed through the crevasses again. Some refugees had not yet returned to their homes; of those who had, many had to abandon an already planted crop of cotton or corn in order to depart once more for tent cities. Economically, the flood area was devastated. Not only had many houses and barns been wrecked, but the crops that could have started people on the road to economic recovery had also drowned, along with much of the livestock.

The crevasse widened and provided relief for New Orleans after diver Ted Herbert placed charges under the water in front of the levee. (National Archives, 77-MRF-173)

3

rescue

The muddy yellow tide respected neither race nor class; it was the common enemy of all living creatures. In one sense people were at their best during the rescue emergency; they sacrificed sleep and regular meals to risk their lives for others. Those who worked hardest in the rescue operation often had the proudest recollections of it, and nearly all agreed that if there were another emergency they would volunteer to join the rescue operation. "I sometimes think that God lets great ca-

Cartoon in the St. Louis *Post-Dispatch,* April 21, 1927, dramatizing the situation in the Mississippi Valley. (Red Cross)

Left to right: James Fieser, Vice Chairman of the Red Cross in charge of domestic operations; Herbert Hoover, Secretary of Commerce and chairman of the President's special flood relief committee; and Dwight F. Davis, Secretary of War. (Red Cross)

lamities fall on us," wrote former Mississippi Congressman and Senator John Sharp Williams a year after the flood, "in order that we may see, realize and *remember* the goodness of the hearts and the generosity of the impulses of our fellow men and women—the spectacle of it, demonstrating in spite of our spells of pessimism and cynicism that we are all, after all, *one*—in spite of differences of section, politics, religion, and race."[1]

Herbert Hoover and James Fieser coordinated the rescue and relief operation. In 1927 Hoover was Secretary of Commerce in President Calvin Coolidge's cabinet and a veteran of relief missions dating from World War I. Trained as an engineer, Hoover used his organizational genius to become a millionaire; his engineering firm did business all over the world. His clockwork mind, able to conceive the intricacies of complex puzzles, immediately grasped the problems of rescue and relief. Hoover's leadership stemmed from his organizational ability; personally he was shy, and so low key that many Mississippians who heard him speak complained that his voice did not carry beyond the first few rows.

James Fieser spent most of his adult life on the front lines of disaster relief. Born in Ravenna, Ohio, he worked in steel mills and plate-glass factories as a young

This rescue craft was powered by a Case threshing machine engine. Herman Caillouet's was powered by a T-Model engine. People in distress exhibited the American characteristic of tinkering to find a way to get the job done. (William A. Percy Library)

man before studying at Indiana University. In 1913 the thirty-year-old Fieser became involved in flood relief work in Columbus, Ohio, and from then until he retired from the Red Cross in 1945 he directed most of its domestic disaster relief. His activities earned him the name "Calamity Jim." "Disasters are nothing new to Red Cross workers," Fieser said on May 1, 1927; "the Galveston flood, the San Francisco earthquake, the great mid-western tornado of 1925, the Northern Ohio tornado of 1924, the South Carolina tornado of 1923, the great Florida hurricane of last September, all lie within their personal experience. But I say unqualifiedly that this flood of the Mississippi and its tributaries by comparison has been far more devastating than any of these disasters."[2]

Most of the rescue work was done by local volunteers. Herman Caillouet rescued nearly two hundred people during the first days of the flood in the Mississippi Delta. For three days he got hardly any sleep as he piloted his T-Model powered boat across the waters, trying to find everyone who was stranded. Caillouet, now in his seventies and still vigorous, in 1927 worked for the U.S. Army Corps of Engineers. "And when you'd stop at the houses to get people, people would get on the boat and dogs or chickens or anything, they would jump in the boat too. Chickens would automatically jump in the boat, see. Course people who had geese and ducks out there, they were happy; they were swimming around. So I started making it from Metcalfe to these Indian Mounds across there. I guess it was about two miles, then, from the Indian Mounds to the main line of the levee, what was left of it.

"One thing I had to do was keep a gun in the boat, cause when your boat got loaded they just keep jumping on there if you wouldn't tell 'em to get off. They wouldn't stand for that. But there were a couple of times I had to raise that gun and say if another one of you jumps in, I'm going to shoot the rest of you off the top of the house. That slowed 'em down."[3]

Joe Simmons of Metcalfe also had a gun in his boat, and he says the only reason he is alive today is that he used it. In 1927 Simmons was a tenant-farmer. He lived near Hollandale, and when the flood waters rolled in he took his boat and tried to get a neighbor's family out of danger. "We had, at least I had, a cow, and if I hadn't had a pistol, that cow would have sunk me. I had this neighbor's family in my boat; he didn't even have a boat. And I made a boat, and I went to get him, and the cow come to the boat. I tried to push back the cow. That cow commenced hollering, that cow was going to come in, so I shot it. That was the only thing that saved us."[4]

Not all rescue stories told in Greenville had happy endings, and Herman Caillouet told of one experience

Skiffs at the Cary, Mississippi, depot. Joe Simmons saved his neighbors in a similar boat. (Corps of Engineers, Vicksburg, 68-AM-335)

that obviously still had its hold on him. "There was a house with seven people on it. I presume it was man and wife and five children. And I was heading over to this house. This was on my first hauling, the next day after the levee broke. And on the way getting to the house, the house was just moving along, you know, all of a sudden it must of hit a stump or something. And the house flew all to pieces. And I searched the boards and things around there for ten minutes, and you know I never saw a soul come up, not a soul. When the house started breaking up and falling, you see, and the waves throwing that lumber over, it just covered 'em to where they couldn't come out from under there, you see. I imagine they could swim. And that's something to see people on top of a house. . . . Must have hit a stump or something and then fall to pieces, and it look like one would have come up. There wasn't a soul that come up. This man and wife, I imagine, seemed to be about thirty-five years old. Oldest kid was, must have been about sixteen."[5]

Virginia Montgomery Pullen, who now lives in Vicksburg, remembers a story that her father told her about the rescue operation in Greenville. Like Herman Caillouet, her father, Hugh Montgomery, was rescuing people near Greenville. "He found one family with two small children, and they handed him the baby out of the tree. It was, I don't know whether she was white or

A house floating down the Sunflower River with a cat as sole survivor. Herman Caillouet saw a family of seven drown when a house disintegrated before his eyes as he attempted to rescue them. (Gordon (Cotton)

Refugees going to the levee along Washington Avenue in Greenville. In the background is Brown's studio, with the familiar Kodak sign displayed. (William A. Percy Library)

black, it wouldn't matter, and two small children and two teenage boys, and he never did know for sure whether they were all in the same family, but she handed him the small baby and just as she handed him the baby, it breathed its last. And, boy, that really upset them recsue workers, him in particular. The idea that they didn't get to her the day before was what he was saying; why didn't we go this far yesterday?"

Virginia Montgomery Pullen was thirteen years old in 1927, but she remembers such incidents as if they happened yesterday. For her, as for many other young people, the flood was an experience that hurled them into the adult world. "I saw my first person die then, from eating too many bananas," she said quietly. "He hadn't had anything to eat in a week, and he came in and they had a boxcar full of bananas, and they had pulled it up to the levee. The man just went in and ate all he could eat. He just stood there and ate a lot of bananas and the next thing you knew, he toppled over dead. We knew him, not real well, but knew him, and it was just horrible. A child to see somebody just eat too much and then drop over, when you knew he hadn't eaten but four or five bananas. For years I wouldn't touch one, which is only natural, I guess."[6]

Nearly everyone connected with the rescue operation seemed to have a special story illustrating how irrational people were in deciding what to salvage from their flooded homes. In most cases refugees just grabbed

The seemingly placid water claimed many victims. Here a mule's ears mark the scene of an overturned wagon. In many cases the water carried the victims to the Gulf of Mexico, making it impossible to ever state accurately how many people drowned. (Corps of Engineers, Vicksburg, 67-AM-174)

what they could, whether it was an ax, a rooster, a victrola, or a trunk.[7]

Frank Hall, an engineer and resident of Greenville, recalled such an incident from his rescue experiences. "We picked up a man and his family out between here and Leland. They were on top of the roof of their house. He was the station agent in the town. He had this chicken farm. We picked him up, brought him to Greenville, and you can't help but notice that people are taking particular care about something. He had a little shoebox on his lap. He was scared to death of the water. No sooner than his foot touched the protection levee, that portion of it next to the main levee (and his name was Bates), he said, 'Gentlemen, I hate to tell you but you'all are going to have to take me back to the house.'

"We said, 'Why?'

" 'I left $400 in my coat pocket of the railroad's money and two diamond rings belonging to my wife hanging up on a nail in the rafters in my attic.'

Refugees in Greenville standing in line for food. To the left is the Mississippi River gauge for Greenville, measuring 45.5. On the same day that the Mound Landing crevasse occurred, it read 54.60. (William A. Percy Library, J. Roscoe Dennis Collection)

In the photograph, handwritten text reads:
"36 IVE Rº ES IN THIS HOUSE HAL TE RET into THE LOFT ACCOUNT RISING WATER. FiRAMY HAD TO CUT HOLE IN THE RºF ACCOUNT WATER STILL RISING AND ALL 36 SOT OUT ON ROOF AND WERE RESCUED. THE OLD COLORED MAN OWNER OF THE HOUSE, PUT LIN CLOTH OVER THE ROOF HOLE. JUST TO KEEP THINGS DRY" PHOTO TAKEN 5 Miles ABOVE MURPHY LANDING... AFAIR 27-1928"

The caption on this picture reads: "36 Negroes in this house had to get into the loft account rising water. Finally had to cut hole in the roof account water still rising and all 36 got out on roof and were rescued. The old colored man owner of the house, put oil cloth over the roof hole, 'just to keep things dry.' " The dog remained behind, as was the case so often. This was taken five miles above Murphy Landing, about 103 miles north of Vicksburg, on April 29. (Gordon Cotton)

"So we said, 'O.K., we'll carry you back, cause your house could wash away. But we're very interested in what it was you were protecting so in that box.'

"He said, 'I'm ashamed to tell you.'

"We said, 'Let's see it.'

"He had twelve little baby chickens."[8]

Many people, of course, had no choice about what they saved, for they emerged with only the clothes on their backs. John E. Montgomery, Virginia Pullen's brother, told the story of a very large black woman who was trapped in her attic, her head protruding through the wooden shingles but her body unable to follow. She had been wedged there for three days when a rescue party heard her screams. When they cut her out, they asked if she had not heard about the approaching high water. She said that she had, but "I didn't know it was gonna be no Norah's flood!"[9]

In order to save people the rescue teams often had to sacrifice animals. A reporter for the Vicksburg *Evening Post* wrote on May 12 that he had seen many touching incidents. "I heard many plead pitifully to be permitted to put their dogs in boats, but this was impossible, and I have seen dogs placed on a board or small rafts and sent off in the current yelping pitifully as they parted forever from their helpless masters who were forced to abandon the faithful animals." Even mules, whom everyone agreed could survive better than horses, hogs, or chickens, sometimes panicked. The Reverend Albert Biever in the *Evening Post* described the fate of some

A dog sitting on the end of the line near Holly Bluff, Mississippi, seemingly resigned to his fate as a victim of the flood. (Red Cross)

mules. "I was told that many of the mules that were driven to the levees became unmanageable and anxious to return to their homes from which they had been driven, jumped into the river and were swept away by the raging current."[10]

A chicken engineered the most spectacular escape from certain drowning. "A White Leghorn rooster, marooned on the roof of a plantation shanty in the flooded district east of Marianna, spied a passing freight train," one newspaper reported. "The cockerel measured the distance and undertook to fly to the train, falling short of his intended terminal about 20 yards. Pressing his ten toes together to form a pair of perfectly good paddles, he headed for the brake rods underneath the box car, the rods clearing the water over the tracks about six inches. The train passed through water but its movement so parted the water that the rooster came through unhurt. When the train stopped on high ground, the cockerel emerged from his roost, shook himself like a wet dog, proudly marched a few steps, threw back his head and crowed a note of victory. The conductor who witnessed the incident caught the bird and took him to his home in Wynne."[11]

That rooster was fortunate, for over a million chickens drowned in the flood, along with 9000 work animals, 26,000 head of cattle, and 127,000 hogs. Meanwhile, the Red Cross fed some 271,000 animals that had reached high ground.

Mules grazing on the levee near Greenville. One flood survivor recalled that the mules "soon ate all the grass and started eating the sandbags." (William A. Percy Library, J. Roscoe Dennis Collection)

"Like a huge retreating army, men, women and children are leaving their homes," reported the Camden *Evening News*. Here mules and automobiles clog the road to high ground. (Red Cross)

The Railroads

In 1927 railroads snaked through the Mississippi Valley; they were a key means of transportation for both people and freight. Usually rails were laid above the flat land on a railroad dump, as they called the roadbed then. During the flood the railroads attempted to keep traffic moving, but in some cases it became impossible, as the waters tore up the track. Many people remember that the tracks looked more like a picket fence than the usually flat railbed. The attempt to save the tracks plus the ruin brought by the flood cost the railroads $10 million, and they contributed another estimated $1.5 million in free transportation and free use of the cars for refugees' homes.

The railroads continued to run as long as the tracks did not wash away. This scene is at Delta Point, Louisiana. The train had just been ferried across the Mississippi River and continued on its way through the rising water. (J. Mack Moore photo, Old Courthouse Museum, Vicksburg, 315)

A scene between Greenville and Leland, Mississippi. The train was still sitting in the same position in July when a relief worker noted that there were two overturned engines, "resting on tracks that have been under water since the levee broke on April twenty-first." (Mississippi Levee Commissioners, Mrs. Horace Polk Collection)

One image that people described continually was of the railroad man, stick in hand, riding on the cowcatcher to push debris out of the way. E. J. Smith, who then lived in Arkansas and worked on the railroad, was one of those who sat on the cowcatcher—but he also remembered that he poked in front of the train to make sure that there was still a track there. He recalled once poking the stick down to see if the track was there as the train crept over the trestle. When asked what he would have done had there been no bridge, he seemed surprised at the question. Smith, like many other volunteers in that time of crisis, did daring things without much thought of the consequences.

Railroad workmen near Tallulah, Louisiana, fight to keep the rails from floating away. (Yerger)

A. H. Blaess of Chicago summed up the contributions of the railroad men in his testimony before Congress in 1927: "Too much cannot be said of the spirit and morale of the men engaged in the stupendous task of protecting and repairing railroads, as the epic story of the work of these men will never be written, due to the fact that as good railroad men they have simply taken it all as a part of the day's work. In sandbagging track, driving bridges through raging torrents, raising track in water—sometimes up to the shoulders—diving under the flood to throw a submerged switch, working long hours under the broiling sun or in driving rain, patrolling miles of water-hidden right of way, both in boats and afoot, the same spirit was evident, regardless of rank."[12]

The tracks near Hamburg, Louisiana, were washed off the roadbed and turned up like a picket fence. (Louisiana Dept. of Public Works)

Refugees taken from high water areas were deposited on this lumber derrick. The *Panther* took 475 refugees off the derrick to make room for 500 more that were on the way. April 24. This was 95 miles north of Vicksburg. (Gordon Cotton)

These were some of the people taken off the Holland Landing Bridge, which was already awash, by the steamer *Ransdell*. (Gordon Cotton)

Because the flood sometimes destroyed the work of a lifetime, not all people could maintain their composure through the ordeal. "To see big, husky, hardhearted men, crying and sobbing like children is to partially realize the terrible shock the flood has wrought," wrote a correspondent from Arkansas City. "Some among those lifted from the housetops had not eaten for four and five days," reported the Memphis *Commercial Appeal*. "Nearly all were thinly clad and were dazed to such an extent that they seemed indifferent about their rescue." Others were not so indifferent. "Reports are coming in hourly of people in the country on tops of houses and trees shooting guns and shouting to attract the attention of some passerby to carry them to safety."

If the flood proved anything about human nature, it showed what people will do in time of disaster. First they helped their families, then their friends, then anyone in danger, and finally they attempted to save animals. "Mr. Thomas is with us," a correspondent aboard a rescue boat observed. "He lost 30 head of mules. We are passing his place and tears are streaming down his face. I heard him say, if only we could save the poor dumb animals—that's what hurts, to see them stand there in the water waiting for death."[13]

One group of heroes in the eyes of many people around Greenville were the bootleggers across the river.

The *C. R. Hull* shoving a barge load of refugees en route to Vicksburg. April 29. (Gordon Cotton)

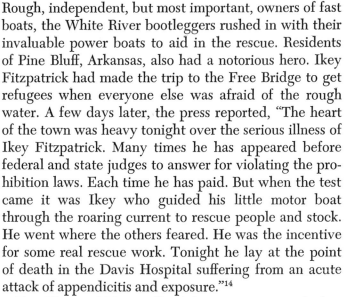

Rescue workers answering a call of distress in Pine Bluff. They were leaving from the back of the Courthouse on their way to Reydell. (Boots Walker)

A cartoon from the Arkansas *Gazette*, May 5, 1927. (Red Cross)

Rough, independent, but most important, owners of fast boats, the White River bootleggers rushed in with their invaluable power boats to aid in the rescue. Residents of Pine Bluff, Arkansas, also had a notorious hero. Ikey Fitzpatrick had made the trip to the Free Bridge to get refugees when everyone else was afraid of the rough water. A few days later, the press reported, "The heart of the town was heavy tonight over the serious illness of Ikey Fitzpatrick. Many times he has appeared before federal and state judges to answer for violating the prohibition laws. Each time he has paid. But when the test came it was Ikey who guided his little motor boat through the roaring current to rescue people and stock. He went where the others feared. He was the incentive for some real rescue work. Tonight he lay at the point of death in the Davis Hospital suffering from an acute attack of appendicitis and exposure."[14]

Eric Hardy of Monticello, Arkansas, ran a car dealership at the time of the flood. When the people from near-by McGehee and the surrounding countryside fled to the hills near Monticello, Hardy and other volunteers drove down to where the hills dissolve into the flat country, fetching refugees to the camp in Monticello. "They thought they were going to lose everthing they had, of course they just had what they could carry and maybe suitcases or in cloth bags or any way they could carry it. I think some of 'em thought maybe we were in the second flood—of the world." Yet the victims were resilient. "When the thing finally began to clear up and we saw the end of the world wasn't right at us, people began thinking about buying cars."[15]

Heroism was not limited to strong men. Five-year-old Iva May Hudnall saved her younger sister. "The younger child fell from a boat which was anchored to their home. As she came up, her older sister grabbed her hair and pulled her to safety."[16]

Commercial Appeal reporter George Moreland found some devoted female workers in Clarendon, Arkansas. "I met two of the three telephone girl heroines. Misses Mabel Renick and Erma Anderson. Miss Rosa Gibson was not present. These young ladies look exactly like modern butterflies. They are dainty, bobbed haired and beautiful. One would think the appearance of a mouse would frighten them and I expect it would; yet, when the angry yellow waters of the White River came roaring through the crevasse not 40 yards from their switchboard, these young ladies sat staunchly and heroically at their place of duty. They never did desert their post. The city has not been without telephone service during its flood. The conduct of these young ladies displays a courage that is remarkable."[17]

Airplanes, probably for the first time in a major disaster, played a rescue role. On April 17 the first sea-

Cartoon in the Brooklyn *Daily Eagle,* May 4, 1927, calling for more boats for the rescue effort. (Red Cross)

In some cases, mule power was more dependable than horsepower. (Red Cross)

plane arrived in Vicksburg, for the personal use of Major John C. H. Lee. Each day he toured the entire line of levees in his district. When the levees began to give way, however, the planes were used to spot refugees. Three seaplanes arrived at Willow Beach near Little Rock on April 22 and fanned out over the flood to search for refugees. It was probably one of these planes that sighted the signals of William Cobb's father.

Most flights were for reconnaissance, to map boat routes, note the progress of the flood, seek refugees, take messages to isolated towns, transport medical supplies, or warn people of the coming flood. Planes hardly ever

A Navy seaplane used for spotting refugees tied to the bank at Vicksburg. Such planes were used for checking for weak places in the levees, delivering mail, and delivering emergency medical supplies. (Illinois Gulf Railroad)

landed in the back country, for the risk of snags was too great. Nor did the planes attempt to rescue people directly; besides other dangers, Lieutenant W. D. Sample reported, "you could not have made a third of the people ride with you in a plane."[18]

Victor Bobb, now retired, in 1927 worked for the Corps of Engineers helping fuel and repair the seaplanes at Vicksburg. "Well, we had thirteen seaplanes up here from Pensacola, and it was my job to keep them planes ready to go. I had a skiff with an outboard motor on it. They couldn't bring them into the bank because the water was about eighteen inches over the railroad track. They couldn't bring them in there with the pontoons. . . . And my job was to keep them gassed up and ready to go." He later flew across the land flooded by the Cabin Teele crevasse, tossing out warning messages to the people below, using a woman's stocking to contain each message and weighting it with a bolt or nut from the machine shop. On that flight he could see the water creeping across the land below. "Ahh, you've seen how fire will go over the ground? Like grass burning? The water was going like that, just creeping. It didn't look like it was real thin; from the air it looked like it might be four or five inches, a wave of it."[19]

The seaplanes received assistance from everyone who was in a position to help. The U.S. Coast Guard participated in the rescue activities, and Boatswain H. S. Browne, Jr., commander of the *Saukee*, reported one in-

Two of the men who flew over the flooded area to report conditions and spot refugees. (Red Cross)

71

cident that revealed the extent of cooperation between the two branches of service. "Seaplanes making reconnaissance over flooded area and threatened levees tied up astern of *Saukee* for refueling; gasoline being secured from supply steamer *U.S. Snag Boat John N. McComb*, moored to trees close to *Saukee's* anchorage. These airmen were assisted every manner possible and occasionally taking dinner on board. On one occasion a member of the crew saw a large water moccasin swimming from the woods. It went directly to seaplane tied up astern, climbed strut and over into the cockpit, hiding in the fuselage. Seaman Hall, armed with a long pair of iron tongs, volunteered to get the snake, and succeeded after two hours' effort. He was quite unassisted, the airmen watching with interest, but refusing to have anything to do with the plane. The snake measured approximately six feet, and it is left to conjecture what would have happened if snake had been discovered while in the air, as the press version of the affair had it."[20]

An airplane flying over Arkansas as the waters receded. (Arkansas History Commission)

"We were flying along the levee about 40 miles south of Baton Rouge over the Germania plantation," wrote Lieutenant George H. Gregory. "I was in the pilot cockpit and Mr. Kilpatrick in the back seat. At about 400 feet, as I was making a turn, something of the machinery controlling the airplane jammed. The machine dove by the nose. All the way down I tried to gain control. When we struck the earth I was thrown completely through the top wing of the airplane. Mr. Kilpatrick was also thrown clear. I was only slightly injured, and I found Mr. Kilpatrick dead as I reached him. I am terribly sorry. The machine was so badly wrecked that we shall never know what happened to it."

Thirty-eight-year-old Earl Kilpatrick had been the General Reconstruction Officer of Mississippi Valley Flood Relief for the American Red Cross. His accidental death on May 30 shocked the Red Cross staff, for he "was the first Red Cross worker to die at the front on emergency duty since the American Red Cross began to write humanitarian history in terms of disaster relief."

His fellow workers recalled Kilpatrick's energy and dedication, a typical pose being "a sandwich in one hand and a telephone receiver in the other." He had worked twenty-hour days for over a month, cataloging facts, directing hundreds of people in rescue and relief work, and was flying to New Orleans for a conference with Director of Relief Henry M. Baker when the seaplane crashed near White Castle, Louisiana.

"He carried his files in his head," a fellow worker remembered. At a meeting five days earlier he had reeled off the "names of 50 or more relief workers in charge of various stations; the number of refugees at each point; the names of boats operating in his area, where they were at the time, whether they were wireless-equipped; details of food shipments; facts; figures; acres; tons; were all paraded before the more or less astonished listeners."

Earl Kilpatrick was born in La Grande, Oregon, and had headed the University of Oregon Extension Division. In 1921, when Pueblo, Colorado, was hit by a flood, the university loaned his services to the Red Cross. Like the university, the Red Cross recognized

Earl Kilpatrick

His fellow workers remembered that this was a characteristic pose as Kilpatrick directed relief efforts in the flood area. *(Red Cross Courier)*

Kilpatrick's tremendous organizational ability; in turn, Kilpatrick realized that he could perform a useful service in times of disaster. "If in the future the Red Cross needs me in any capacity in any major disaster," he promised then, "I will not hesitate to answer its call." For five years he did answer the call, supervising several disaster relief operations and then returning to his duties at the University of Oregon. In 1926 he resigned his duties at the university to become a full-time Red Cross staff member. As the relief work continued in the Mississippi Valley after his death, the flag at National Red Cross Headquarters in Washington flew at half-mast.[21]

Formal portrait of Kilpatrick. (Red Cross, *The Mississippi Flood Disaster of 1927*)

M. W. Rasmussen, District Commander of the Fifth Coast Guard District, boasted that the "shooting of the crevasses by the power surfboats was probably as spectacular as anything that happened during the entire operations. The slope of the crevasse varied from a few feet to thirty feet, the water rushing through at a rate in proportion to the slope. Invariably three crested waves formed at the foot of the slope. As soon as sufficient water had flowed through the crevasse to prevent possibility of boat grounding at the foot of the slope, the power surfboats would square away and glide through, oftentimes at an estimated speed of forty miles per hour. Upon striking the waves at the foot of the slope the boats would partly fill up but immediately free themselves upon passing through. Upon one occasion, in negotiating a crevasse at Bordelonville Boatswain Sam Carlson jumped his power surfboat completely out of water when striking the waves at the foot of the slope."

Shooting the crevasses was spectacular and dangerous, but much of the duty proved to be exhausting. Rasmussen praised his men for their cooperation and fortitude. "The men bore up wonderfully well under the strain. It often became necessary for them to sleep in their boats or on the levee without adequate protection from mosquitoes. As a preventative against malaria fever which was prevalent, quinine was issued to all hands. In many cases the men were so badly bitten by mosquitoes as to be unrecognizable or unable to get their shoes on. Rather than to expose themselves many of the men put

Volunteer rescue workers along the Bayou des Glaises near Marksville. At the extreme right is Father Van de Putten. (Paul Coco)

One of the Coast Guard surfboats with a load of refugees near Marksville. (Paul Coco)

The genius of the rescue operation, Lieutenant Colonel George S. Spalding. He directed all operations. On the wall behind him is a map of the Mississippi River. (Red Cross)

on boots and oilskins before turning in for the night as a preventative against mosquito bites. Yet there was not a single complaint."

When a telephone call of distress reported cries of help downriver at two in the morning, twenty men volunteered for the mission, and, according to Rasmussen, "in less than an hour a rescue party in charge of Boatswain J. Daly and Boatswain McInnis of the C.B. 251 were enroute to the trouble. At 7:00 a.m. the party returned after having rescued 20 persons whose power boat had run aground on a sand bar in the river."

"In another instance," Rasmussen continued, "when the Melville bridge was carried away, the bridge tenders, a father and his son, were carried away with it. A Coast Guard crew seeing the bridge go down and knowing that there were men on it, immediately started down the rapidly moving current in search of the men who had been on the bridge. They were successful in saving one life, that of the son, the father was evidently caught in the bridge house as he did not come to the surface of the water. Incidentally this was the only life lost to the knowledge of the undersigned in the entire area in which the Coast Guard operated."[22]

The rescue operation proceeded in stages, and often there was another trip in store for refugees after their initial rescue. Small boats fanned out from larger ones

A pile of boats awaiting volunteers. The railroads delivered the boats to where they were most needed. (Red Cross)

and returned full of refugees, to the larger ships; when these became full, they journeyed to the refugee camps.

Although most refugees made a simple transition from housetop to boat to levee, others from more isolated areas had to board barges or larger boats for a longer trip to a refugee camp. This added to their distress. "One aged man who had lost very heavily," reported a Coast Guard captain, "attempted to jump overboard. He had to be guarded by four men throughout the trip." On the other hand, the same commander reported that "a bevy of twenty flappers captured the crew who blew them to a special cooked dinner after the others had been served, and otherwise extended courtesies which were well received." Always, in the relief work and in the camps, there was the juxtaposition of despair and happiness.[23]

Boatswain H. S. Browne, Jr., commander of the *Saukee*, reported that his ship was probably "the first seagoing cutter ever put in at Baton Rouge." The visit was so special that Browne was received at the governor's mansion. The *Saukee* quickly went into action on the Red River and 347 refugees, most from the Bayou des Glaises area of Louisiana, gathered on board.

"It developed that among the refugees was a boy with broken leg that had been unset for over a day. Also a baby with pneumonia and its mother was sick. In ad-

A volunteer Red Cross worker pausing for a photo in the Bayou des Glaises area. (Red Cross)

"Just completing three weeks service in the sugar-bowl basin of Louisiana. At Plaquemine, Louisiana, Locks on June 6, 1927," was the caption on this photo. These are Coast Guard surfboats. (Red Cross)

dition two other mothers were found ill." Instead of putting the refugees aboard another boat, Browne proceeded directly to Baton Rouge. "The passengers were well distributed about the deck, women and children given choice of stern of boat and boat deck near chart house. Those with babies were placed in the wardroom together with boy having broken leg. The sick mothers and babies were assigned to the cabin, colored women to mess room and other colored refugees on forecastle or along inside rail." There were 267 whites and 80 blacks aboard, and the ship's crew served them water, coffee, and sandwiches.

"But on the Mississippi a cold raw wind was met with," Browne continued, "and there was a tendency on part of some to make for lee rail. This was prevented without any trouble. In fact, the majority seemed so apathetic as a result of their losses that it is doubted if they would have moved if the decks were flooded. . . . Numerous articles of bedding were on the forecastle and also many colored people. But as the cold increased, the people disappeared until hardly one was in sight or sign of life except an occasional lurching mattress or moving pile of bed clothes. But to negotiate a passage required extreme care; a foot would be protruding here, a hand there, or you might find your foot right over a child's face. . . . A glimpse in the cabin disclosed five infants in the bunk, three women and four other babies taking up most of the floor space. . . . By time *Saukee* was well on her way, all had quieted down with an occasional service here and there. An encouraging word to a few anxious ones. . . . Arriving Baton Rouge, found ambulance and Red Cross man there in response to radio and berth already arranged for by *Commanche*. All refugees were landed and with their luggage, bedding and other trappings had departed for their quarters in an hour's time."[24]

The men assigned to the surfboats did not have such plush accommodations, for they were out in the rough water snatching refugees where they could find them. Their daring rescue work cut down on drownings. Boatswain Clifford C. Lee reported on some of the activities of Coast Guard Boat 225 out of Biloxi, Mississippi:

"Boatswain Kinkade, C. B. M. Rosser, Bos'n M. 1c Lewis arrived at home at 11 p.m., breaking through upper loft and rescuing one woman with two hour's old baby and 5 other small children; carried them to safety on stretchers; the house being washed away a few minutes afterward. This is one of several serious cases we had to contend with, finding some partly paralized and unable to walk; and moving them on stretchers. . . .

"There were several families moved from lofts and house tops, some being blocked up on scaffolds. This was the worst sight ever witnessed by any of these men. Though they met the condition of old timers and worked faithfully throughout the flood. No one showed any signs of being dissatisfied and all seemed in good spirits.

"The negro and the whites were cared for the same, all having the best of care that could be given on a small boat. There was several times they did not have standing room, being put in one position and having to remain that way until we reached camp."[25]

On June 16 H. H. Wolf, commander of the Coast

The coordination of the rescue operation is shown in this photo, taken near Simmesport, Louisiana. Surfboats brought refugees from the flooded areas to be put on the larger boats. The *Saukee*, the seagoing cutter on the right, was taking refugees aboard for a trip to Baton Rouge, while the riverboat *Kankakee* stood by for other refugees. Boatswain H. S. Browne, Jr., gave a vivid account of his trip to Baton Rouge. (Red Cross)

The paddlewheeler *Sprague,* a towboat owned by Standard Oil Company, pushing a barge loaded with refugees to Vicksburg. Virginia Montgomery Pullen made her trip from Greenville to Vicksburg on such a barge. "A lot of people were crying," she remembered. (Gordon Cotton)

Guard's Gulf Division, attempted to sum up the operations. "In a campaign such as this has been," he observed, "where every man, so far as I have been able to learn, rendered the most willing, faithful, and tireless service, and in which there were undoubtedly many unheralded performances of high deed, the singling out of individuals for special mention is a matter to induce hesitation, in the interest of exact justice. I suppose it is always understood that special mention does not, nor can not, detract from the merit of another man." After saying all this, two of the men he recognized for merit were Boatswain C. C. Lee, in charge of CG 225, and Boatswain H. S. Browne, Jr., commander of the *Saukee.*[26]

When the flood came to Greenville, Virginia Montgomery and her family fled to the courthouse, where she stayed the first night before moving to the second story of another building. After several weeks of living in this

80

manner, she boarded the *Sprague* for a trip down river to Vicksburg, where they would all stay with relatives until the flood receded at Greenville and the house was cleaned up. (She later married the man who became one of the great pilots of the *Sprague*, Jap Pullen.)

"They put Momma and my grandfather and the two smaller children on the inside of the *Sprague*. I don't remember where, but the bigger children, and of course I thought I was grown too, we were to stand on the barges, you know, get out on the barges. They had something like chicken wire around it so we wouldn't fall in the river, but they had this thing built around it and we stood out there. I guess maybe we had some way to sit down or something, but we were on the boat overnight. We didn't have a place to sleep either, except out on the barge. And they served us sandwiches. We tried to sing. I'm sure everyone was off-key. But we sang as long as you could, and everybody tried to tell where they were from. A lot of people were crying; I remember that. A lot of people.

"We got to Vicksburg, and you know people in Vicksburg think these are hills; to me this will always be a mountainous part of the world, because these were the tallest mountains in the world—because I'd seen too much water."[27]

refugees

"They called us refugees," Cora Lee Campbell recalled, with obvious distaste for the word. "That's what they called, and I guess that's what we were." When asked how she fared in the Deeson, Mississippi, relief camp, she replied, "I tell you, some places, some time, hit was hard. I'm going just going to tell the truth. Sometimes hit was hard." Verna Reitzammer's reply was quite different. "It was like living in Venice to me, and of course riding around in the boats. And of course there was just plenty going on. We danced and sang and enjoyed the town." That Arkansas City for a young white woman was different from a tent city in Mississippi for a young black woman with a child emphasizes the dissimilarity of experience among the flood refugees. Yet beneath the despair and the happiness there was a common understanding that the flood was a great catastrophe. "To ride in a motorboat down between those trees was real pretty," Verna Reitzammer added, "if you didn't stop to think what was going under."[1]

In Mississippi, Arkansas, and Louisiana over 14 million acres were flooded, driving nearly 600,000 people from their homes. Nearly half of these refugees found shelter in upper stories of buildings, some in their own homes, and many of those who could afford to feed themselves did so. The main burden of relief, however, fell on the Red Cross. The 307,280 people in the camps in those three states ate food and lived in tents and houses furnished by that organization; it also fed 288,600 people who lived outside the camps, and in the other states affected by the flood it fed over 41,000 people.

Red Cross workers first had to decide where to put the relief camps. Not all decisions were as easy as the one to establish four refugee camps at the national park in Vicksburg. On the hills far above the river the 15,000 refugees were safe from the flood waters; they had a large, sprawling park for the tents, and rail and river lines were open to bring in food. Throughout the valley there were 154 refugee camps, 129 of them in Mississippi, Louisiana, and Arkansas. In some cases it was difficult to find a site with good drainage and access to

Arkansas City. The Desha Bank and Trust Co. building. The fire engine to the left of the boardwalk went under, though the town fathers thought it would be safe so close to the levee. (Verna Reitzammer)

84

supplies, but only a few camps presented a health hazard.

Taken as a whole, the performance of the professional Red Cross staff and the volunteers who worked with them is one of the most noble relief efforts in the history of the nation. And people all over the country joined in the effort; private contributions eventually amounted to

Refugees posing for photographer J. Mack Moore in Vicksburg before heading for the refugee camp on the hills above. (J. Mack Moore Collection, Old Courthouse Museum, Vicksburg, 312)

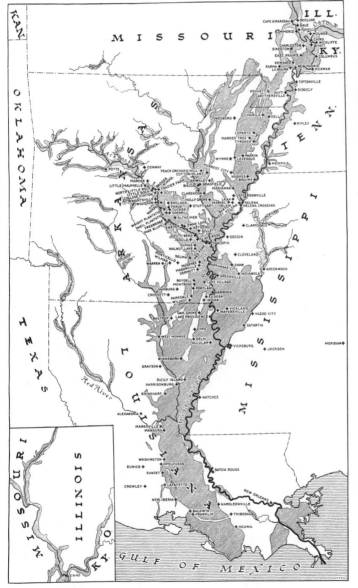

Approximate areas flooded by Mississippi River and Tributaries in seven states during 1927. This shows location of Red Cross emergency relief camps. (Red Cross, *The Mississippi Valley Flood Disaster of 1927*)

On the hills above Vicksburg some 15,000 refugees huddled waiting for the flood waters to subside. It was an ideal setting for a refugee camp. (Corps of Engineers, Vicksburg, 67-AM-128)

The DeKalb County, Georgia, chapter of the Red Cross collecting flood donations in a fair booth in Decatur. (Red Cross Courier, July 1, 1927, p. 20)

The Red Cross raised over $17 million for flood relief. The *Red Cross Courier* reported on this effort by quoting from the children who staged a play to raise funds. "We worked awful hard to get the $3.12 and wee hope it helps the flood victims," wrote the twelve youngsters involved in the "Big Show." "For ammission we got rags & paper & nickels. We sold the rags & paper to the rag man. Our mothers made candy that we sold in between the acts." *(Red Cross Courier,* July 1, 1927, p. 7)

$17,498,902.16, and another $6,129,000 in support came from the various governmental agencies, railroads, and state governments. There were also miscellaneous gifts in food and clothes.

Because of the overwhelming success of the Red Cross in the rescue, relief, and rehabilitation operation, some statements made by Hoover, Fieser, and some Red Cross executives defy explanation. Perhaps Hoover, who was beginning to groom himself for the 1928 presidential race, feared that even a slight blemish in his flood relief role would mar his political appeal (although time and again he said that flood relief was not political). Fieser and the Red Cross, counting on voluntary contributions by the American people, feared that contributions might fall off if certain conditions were publicized. Whatever the reason, official reports and press releases failed to mention some very important developments in the relief camps and insisted continually that only about six people had drowned since the Red Cross had organized the rescue operation. Exaggerating the success of the rescue was one thing; ignoring a venereal disease epidemic for weeks and refusing to publicize conditions of peonage were serious and puzzling omissions.

At some point in his relief work, Herbert Hoover seized upon the statistic that only a half-dozen people

25 PEOPLE DROWNED JUMPING FOR LIVES

Refugee Population Doubles Town's Normal Demand.

MORE BOATS ARE NEEDED

MEMPHIS BOY DROWNS WHEN BOAT OVERTURNS

Roger Yates, Telephone Lineman, Is Victim.

THREE OTHERS LOSE LIVES

FARM HANDS PERISH AT SCOTT CREVASSE

Furious Waters of Mississippi Trap Negro Laborers.

EIGHTEEN LOST WHEN BOAT IS DRAWN INTO LEVEE BREAK, REPORT

Launch Pelican Goes Down at Knowlton's Landing.

LOADED WITH REFUGEES

All on Board Believed to Have Perished.

had drowned after the Red Cross organized rescue, clinging to it despite all contrary evidence. "To have moved 400,000 people from their homes under these dangerous circumstances," he told a nationwide radio audience on May 18, "and to have accomplished it with but loss of less than six lives is the monument to their effectiveness and their courage." The effectiveness and the courage of the rescue volunteers was obvious, but "less than six lives" was simply untrue. Yet he continued to repeat the statistic throughout the spring and summer, and by January 1928 he had not changed his figures when he wrote his prepared statement for an appearance before a congressional committee: "Owing to the fine organization and energy displayed by the Red Cross and Governmental departments, there were actually less than half a dozen lives lost by drowning after the organization was set up." Hoover made that statement despite having received a letter from DeWitt Smith of the Red Cross: it warned that, "Our figures on drowning are not necessarily reliable, nor do we have anything to show the number of persons drowned after the relief work was definitely organized on a centralized basis."

Hoover dated his "half a dozen" estimate from the time when the Red Cross took over control of rescue and relief, "within a few days after the first break of the levee at Dorena," which occurred on April 16. Yet five days later nineteen people were drowned when the launch *Pelican* was caught in a huge eddy and went through a crevasse near Helena, Arkansas. There were often unsubstantiated rumors of drownings, but the *Pelican* disaster was confirmed by the Corps of Engineers.

Even if Hoover began his count from the time of organized relief following the Mound Landing crevasse on April 21, the number of drownings rapidly outran his "half a dozen." The victims of the *Pelican* aside, and discounting an unconfirmed rumor of twenty-five victims of a tragedy in Leland, and omitting those who drowned when the Mound Landing levee broke, between April 24 and April 30 the Memphis *Commercial Appeal* reported that some sixty-three people had

88

Some donations were food and clothes. This train brought food for people and stock to Stoneville, Mississippi. (Red Cross)

A cartoon from the Milwaukee *Journal,* April 22, 1927. (Red Cross)

This document describes the death of four refugees on April 30 on their way to Vicksburg. (Red Cross Archives)

STATEMENT MADE BY W.C. GORDON.

We were at Onward, Mississippi Depot, when boat passed there. We were asked " if we wanted to come to Vicksburg?" and we replied "Yes". They said " We are fixing our lines and are going into Vicksburg some time tonight." We answered " That is perfectly all right ".

When we got to Valley Park, Lee got aboard. He had a gallon of whiskey in his trunk. Some of the boys said " Gosh! I wish I had a drink." Lee said " I have a gallon in my trunk. Go and get it ". They did and took two or three drinks.

B.B. Mullun, scared and half-sick took the whiskey and hid it. When they asked for the whiskey he told them he didn't know where it was. They kept begging for the whiskey and said they were going to tie the boat up if they didn't get it. So after they got the whiskey and took another drink, we pulled into the Yazoo River at the Illinois Central Bridge. Come on up the railroad a piece and started running. Took another drink and then almost hit a cattle house floating down the River. He made around it all right and then pulled the motor wide open.

We passed into Steele Bayou. We looked far ahead and saw a steam boat, and I told them to take the far edge so we could make it all right around this boat. I began unlacing my shoes as I was uneasy. He began to blow the whistle when we got even with the large boat. The large boat did not shut down. When we passed the big boat large waves were thrown over. Our boat with engine still wide open hopped over a large wave and went under.

B.B. Mullan had one Life Saver and I had the other. The only two on the boat. I took the Life Saver and give it to Mr. Lee. I told him " I can swim, you take the Life Saver ". He took it and standing on the bow of the boat when I left him with Clem Mullen. I asked Clem if he could swim and he said he could a little, so I told him to stay with me and I would help him. We were going to a Fisherman's boat when the current hit us. I had a dog with me. I went on to the Fisherman's boat and hollered back to him, but heard no sound. He had gone under.. When the current hit me I was 200 yards XXXXX from a tree and about 200 to 250 yards from the Fisherman's boat. When I reached the tree and climbed same, I hollered again, but got no answer.

B.B. Mullen was in the water holding to a twig. He asked " Do you know where the others are?" and I replied " They are on the other side" which we passed him (Mullen). I told him to hold still and we would be back after him, but current was so swift, we couldn't stop.

We went as far as we could, then hollered finally picked up four men, counting myself and Mullen made the fifth man. The Fisherman took us to his cabin, gave us lodging for the night and we arrived in Vicksburg this morning at 6;30 A.M.

X Florence Groome   X W.C. Gordon

X J. Garrett

A crippled refugee sitting beside his trunks waiting for the waters to subside. (Red Cross)

drowned in the flood. Other newspapers throughout the flood area confirmed this figure. During May, as the flood rushed south, drownings continued in Louisiana. Even Red Cross documents confirm this. Of the 237 people who drowned in the flood, the 16 in Louisiana and certainly many of the 78 in Arkansas and 125 in Mississippi perished after the Red Cross took over the rescue work. But Hoover never retracted his "half a dozen" claim nor did he so much as hint that he was using a totally false figure. Because he was often in the

The water was running-
board high on these trucks
and cars in Rolling Fork,
Mississippi. (Illinois Central
Gulf Railroad)

flood area, he had to have known that it was inaccurate.
The question still remains: why did he choose to repeat it?[2]

Those who survived the threat of drowning were
mostly rural people accustomed to acres and acres of
land stretching before them; for them the shock of in-
stant urbanization in a relief camp was unsettling.
Spring planting was due, but the fertile lands were inundated; farmers, impatient to get at the task, were
sentenced by the flood to spend weeks, sometimes
months, in enforced leisure. There was also apprehension: the refugees did not know if their houses remained, or their furnishings, or their implements. Many
observers reported a look of alienation on the faces of
refugees, a gaze distant and sad.

When refugees stepped off the rescue boats, they en-
countered a routine quite different from their usual life.
By the same token, the volunteer relief workers were also
apprehensive about their new jobs. Mrs. Waggaman
Berl gave an account of her experiences as the first refugees landed in Vicksburg on Easter Sunday. "While I
was in the office a large boat was seen steaming down
the river with two enormous barges and the barges
fairly alive with humanity. Some one grasped my hand
and said, 'Are you doing anything? Come, we'll go
down and help feed them and register them.' So we

With the streets under water in Tallulah, Louisiana, R. C. Lewis piloted Dr. Gaines as he made a house call. (Corps of Engineers, Vicksburg, 67-AM-147)

Two photographs taken in Vicksburg on April 23 as refugees arrived from the flooded Delta. Such scenes must have been familiar to Mrs. Waggaman Berl as she registered and cared for the refugees. (Gordon Cotton)

dashed down the very steep hill to the water front. There I was put to work at registering this huge load of refugees. Those who were not totally exhausted with the exposure of the long cold night on the open barge climbed off and registered at the railway station nearby. But there were many others too weary and ill to move.

"This registration was one of the first of the many splendid and efficient schemes instituted by the Red Cross. Every refugee was 'card indexed' the minute he arrived. His or her name, how many in the family, where they were from, who they worked for in that town, and whether they were in need of assistance from the Red Cross. Many women and children were sent to us, their husbands being retained for work on the local levees. Later when their husbands followed them, their first inquiry would be, 'Where can I go to find my wife and children?' We could always tell them where to go to join their kin. Every registered person was given a duplicate card to present whenever they asked for clothes, food, or space in the tents. The card identified the bona fide refugees and discouraged local people from using Red Cross facilities.

"This was the first boatload that I had registered—about 1,200 refugees. Most of them were in a pitiable condition. The weather had grown bitter cold. I was wearing winter clothes and a coat, yet all the children were barefooted and most of them wore no underclothing. They were all coughing and some had fevers.

"Frequently they carried very elaborate and gay patchwork quilts—the kind that bring such high prices in New England antique shops today."[3]

Home demonstration workers also volunteered to work on the filing system, and R. S. Wilson, director of extension work in Mississippi, added to Mrs. Berl's description. "This was indeed, a gigantic and depressing task," he explained in his report. "It was here that people appeared from day to day frantically searching for their loved ones, from whom they had been separated by the high water, and in some cases, death or insanity. It took nerve to tell a man that the wife for whom he had been searching was in the insane asylum, having been taken there as soon as she arrived at Camp."[4]

An unidentified refugee camp. Mrs. Waggaman Berl reported that the refugees frequently "carried very elaborate and gay patchwork quilts—the kind that bring such high prices in New England antique shops today." Note the quilts on the lines in the foreground. (Illinois Central Gulf Railroad, in Hoover Library, Album 5-00171A)

Red Cross workers and other volunteer relief personnel realized that the biggest problem in relief camps was boredom. Refugees in Vicksburg played volleyball. (Red Cross)

Across the flooded area, volunteers attempted to find some way to relieve the depression and boredom of relief camps. Demonstration workers, accustomed to showing people how to perfect their canning, sewing, quilting, and other domestic skills, found in the refugees a field ripe unto the harvest. Some workers explained that they had never come in contact with people from these hinterland areas in their regular rounds. R. S. Wilson described some of the work done in Vicksburg. "Regular sewing classes were held in all the camps, including such instruction as making over garments, use of simple patterns, use of sewing machine, and short cuts in sewing. The Singer Sewing Machine

94

Company cooperated most generously by lending machines for use in the camps.

"Demonstrations were also given in rug making, piecing of quilts, mattress making, refinishing of old furniture and floors. These were of real assistance to those who expected to return to devastated homes.

"For children in the camps, they conducted story hours, games, and songs. At Camp Whitfield 4000 tooth brushes were received from the Takamine Company, Trenton, N.J., which were distributed to both the negro and white children. Under the direction of the Home Demonstration Agent, several Natchez school children gave demonstrations in brushing the teeth."[5]

Up the river in Greenville, before she boarded the *Sprague* for Vicksburg, Virginia Montgomery found refugee life in a second story adventuresome, but sometimes sobering. "Daddy wouldn't let us go into the house," she remembered. "I went once; he carried us one time and I saw my shoes on the mantle floating around. I had begged him so to buy them for my birthday, and he said, all right, I'll get 'em but you can't wear 'em till then. I never did get to wear them high heels. You know, I've never cared for them since then. That was, I guess, a twist of fate. That just really turned me against them, but I wanted them so bad then, you know. You think you're grown when you're thirteen.

"The first time we went in there we saw a big snake in our living room and the next day my daddy went in. I wasn't with him, and he went in, and there was a col-

Children standing in line for milk in Vicksburg. (Red Cross)

Virginia Montgomery Pullen's family lived in this upper story for several weeks before moving downriver to Vicksburg to live with relatives. In the boat on the right is Virginia's father, R. H. Montgomery, and next to him her grandfather, H. V. Pulliam. In the left window above, peering out of the shadows, are Thomas and Robert. Virginia is looking over Bessie's shoulder. Sitting on the ledge in the center window is Mrs. R. H. Montgomery. John, three years old at the time, saw his dog fall out of the window onto the awning and drown in the flood waters, and later John fell out of a boat and was rescued by guardsmen. Here he is at his mother's knee. The other people are members of another family that stayed in the back part of the building during the flood. (William A. Percy Library)

Flood scene in Greenville. Despite the high water, people attempted to settle into some routine, either sitting on the front gallery of a store or riding wagons through the "Queen City of the Delta." (Corps of Engineers, Vicksburg, 68-AM-341)

ored man floating in the same living room. He had just floated in there, and he had gotten wedged.

"After, I would say four days, my future brother-in-law rode a horse in. How far is it to Wayside, ten miles? He rode and swam a horse in town to see if my sister was still living, right through the flood. He went on the levee part of the way, and then when he got to town, he went to the house. He began asking, and somebody told him we were on the corner. You know, a girl of thirteen thinks of a white knight coming on a horse, and boy, I thought this was the greatest thing. This horse was swimming and Clyde Durham was on it. My sister is three years older than me; she was sixteen. They finally got married."[6]

As much as a second story, boxcar, or tent city facilities allowed, people attempted to reestablish a routine. They wanted a link between the old existence and the new; they needed some familiar pattern. Many of the black refugees had saved their victrolas and listened to favorite records. Some of the other refugees had saved nothing at all—except their lives. For others the refugee camps were vacation resorts. In normal times few farm workers in the flood area had the leisure to attend the movies, but they did in many refugee camps, where

Riding high. G. Ramsey Russell, the young man at the left, saved this picture of a heavily modified Dodge automobile that his father, at the right with the straw hat, built to navigate the flood waters in Greenville. (Mississippi Levee Commissioners, G. Ramsey Russell Collection)

movies were shown each evening. Medical attention was better in the camps than where they worked, food was at least comparable to the plantation fare, tents rivaled cabins for comfort, and leisure was not a problem for everyone. In a few days or weeks there emerged a new routine, one born of necessity.

Perhaps the psychological adjustment was most difficult, for independent farming people were not accustomed to asking for relief—only for credit. Lugenia B. Christmas, a home demonstration agent from St. Francis County, Arkansas, told of a woman who came into Forrest City to seek shelter. "As we entered a large building, a ware house, in which 150 families were being housed, a mother, Rebecca Brown, by name, from Round Pond, a club member, who was in our last demonstration on April 13th, met us with water streaming from her clothing, and also her two boys, 4 and 7 years respectively, whom she held by the hands. She said that she and her children had waded water from three miles and came on wagon the remaining part of the way, in the rain, and the few articles of clothing that she brought were all water soaked. She said: 'We are wet, cold and hungry and have been since yesterday. Have not had a bite to eat since yesterday morning. Yet, I'll make out, if you'll only help me to get something to eat and some dry clothes for my children, and there's my sister with her little boy 9 years old in the same fix.' "[7]

No matter where people fled, they tried to carve out a new home. Here refugees living in an Illinois Central box car managed to establish a front porch, a washline, screen doors, and even had some plants near by to remind them of home. (Yerger)

This temporary refugee home in Blanton, Mississippi, was barely above the water. (Mississippi Levee Commissioners)

The "Willis House," an Illinois Central caboose in Rolling Fork, Mississippi. (Illinois Central Gulf Railroad)

Maude Maddox, who lived near Lake Village, Arkansas, at the time of the flood, did not like camp life at Eudora. "In the first place, I never cared too much about big crowds. And with two children. I had one that was about three and a half and one toddler. In the afternoons, I would read to any child who wanted to come and listen to me. But the meals, I had never been used to a thing like that. We'd have to go by that [she mimiced a person dishing out food] in the canteen. We had a tent. Now the sleeping arrangements were nice. We had our own tent, the children and I. It was big for three people. We had three cots. I didn't have a bit of complaint there. It was rather interesting, because we had people all around us. But still we could have our own little family there. We could go in the afternoon to town; we walked of course. The bathing facilities were rather crude. And with two children, that bath is necessary.

"And we got up and just did what we wanted to," she said, describing a typical day. "Then about, I guess eight o'clock we had breakfast. And it took us quite a long while in line. . . . Then after that we had our noon meal, but they didn't have any planned things. I didn't stay down there very long, really not long enough to get in the thick of things. Oh, they would drop the mail. That was a big deal, from the airplane. Somebody was there nearly every day to talk to the people. I think they were restless. It was a new experience for everybody. It was just the uneasiness of things, like a war. . . . I had some friends who lived in Eudora, and they came out twice to visit. So it wasn't bad, but I was really, really glad to get home."[8]

The emergency put people who normally lived routine lives on the front line of rescue, relief, and care for the refugees. Many of the home demonstration agents who had spent their time touring a county showing women how to can, sew, and keep house discovered a new world that the flood had washed up. Dora S. Stub-

Nurse Porter caring for Mrs. D. P. Achen of Braithwaite, Louisiana, in the New Orleans refugee camp. (Red Cross)

A few "bed things" airing out in the Mansura, Louisiana, refugee camp. Rural people, accustomed to the wide spaces of farm life, found it very difficult to adjust to the cramped conditions in a tent city. (Paul Coco)

101

Many refugees complained that the food was slopped onto their plates and mixed to the point where it was tasteless. Cora Lee Campbell, after forty-eight years, claimed that the poorly prepared and badly served food at the Deeson, Mississippi, refugee camp destroyed her taste. Here refugees eat at the Birdsong Camp in Cleveland, Mississippi. (Illinois Central Gulf Railroad, in Hoover Library, Album 6-00043)

blefield from Craighead County, Arkansas, wrote of these new experiences in her flood report. "To start with I worked in the refugee camp five days. This gave me an opportunity to study the type of people. It was here where I first realized they were the class I could not or did not reach in club work. Also I could see defects in children caused from lack of proper feeding. At the camp I issued clothing as help was scarce and, too, the people could not be gotten together very easily as they were so upset over leaving their homes. Besides the water was not so high in this county that they had to be in camp very long, only a few days."[9]

But there were frustrations, and Geraldine Green Orrell reported some of the problems in Poinsett County, Arkansas. "Contentions between Red Cross nurses and the County Health Officers here resulted in few typhoid inoculations being given here and no malaria treatments were given. However, I finally got the health officer to agree to give prescriptions for those having chills, I got a druggist here to agree to handle the quinine and I went to Marked Tree to the Red Cross Nurse, got the

It was not all boredom in McGehee, Arkansas. These men engaged in a little horseplay. (Desha Public Library)

102

quinine and gave it to the druggist; thus malaria will be treated."[10]

Albert Tilbury, now a park ranger at the Chemin-A-Haut State Park near Bastrop, Louisiana, was fourteen years old when his family fled Wilmot, Arkansas, in 1927. "That's the year that we brought all them mules. We was coming out of Wilmot with 'em and when they hit the bayou bridge, it's, I guess, 300 feet, no more than that, but anyhow it was just a steel-wooden bridge and a ten ton limit is what they got on 'em. But when all them mules got on that doggone bridge, I was just scared and that water was all the way up and clean up over the road, and it was slapping against that bridge. I just happened to make the remark, I said, 'Look out, That whole daggone bridge, mules and all, goin' to sink.' That's the first thing I thought about. I never will forget that. And it just scared the hell out of them men. They got up there and helped them mules; they didn't let that bridge get that full no more.

"Stock drowned and you never seen as many snakes and stuff in all your life; there was all kinds of snakes. They would get right up in the boat with you if you'd let 'em. They didn't bite hardly, unless you get one hemmed up, or stepped on him. You got to be messing with him to make him bite you.

The diet of many tenant farmers in the flooded area was not balanced. A home demonstration agent in Arkansas reported, "I could see defects in children caused from lack of proper feeding." These children waited for milk to supplement their diet. (Red Cross)

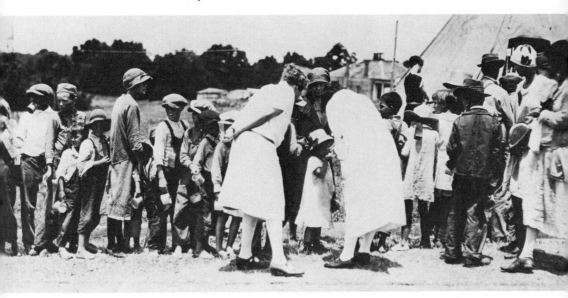

"It was muddy, and just everything in the world floating. You could see all kinds of household goods, dead chickens, dead pigs, dead cows and everything else was floating in that water.

"They come up here with families, just like dad. Now he had eight or ten colored families on the place and two or three white families. Well, they all come up here with us, and we all stayed in the Deep Creek school house, and everybody cooked together and eat together, you know what I mean? I couldn't tell no difference in the eating. I just enjoyed it 'cause I was a kid. One day, all them farmers got together and they had about seventy-five or a hundred head of bull yearlings out there in that bunch of cattle that they brought up here. Well, they all got together, and they castrated all them cattle, them bulls. They called 'em mountain oysters. And they cooked them things. And I helped 'em, and I said, shoot, I don't believe I'll eat them things. And they got them things cooked, and I ate one of 'em, and good god, you talk about good! I couldn't get enough of 'em. Man you talk about good! Them bull nuts is good to eat. Man, they eat hog nuts and bull nuts and all back then.

In Arkansas some local volunteers discovered it was difficult to find support for inoculation, but Birdie Weems, a Red Cross nurse from Little Rock, did her job. (Red Cross)

I see chit'lins in the store now and then, but I never see no mountain oysters in the stores."[11]

During May, as refugees were getting accustomed to camp life, pressure from black leaders throughout the land forced Herbert Hoover to appoint a "Colored Advisory Commission" to investigate complaints that tenants were being held in peonage in some refugee camps. Simply put, peonage is debt servitude, a form of slavery that existed side by side with legitimate sharecropping arrangements. By 1927 there had been three major Supreme Court cases and numerous other federal cases dealing with peonage, so it was not obscure. It had been well publicized. During the flood planters feared

Mules and people huddling on the railroad dump in Leland. This photo was taken from the water tank looking north. (Mississippi State Archives)

The Colored Advisory Commission. Robert R. Moton is third from the right in the first row, Claude Barnett is second from the left in the first row, Thomas M. Campbell is last on the right in the back row, and Jesse O. Thomas is third from the right in the back row. (Red Cross)

that laborers would leave the area for more lucrative jobs elsewhere, leaving them short of help. Although no court case was brought to establish whether the relief camps served in effect as prisons where debt-ridden workers were held against their will, there is evidence that such was often the case. Like so many peonage arrangements, the compulsion was so subtle that not even the victim knew whether his condition was free or slave. The commission, headed by Robert Russa Moton, president of Tuskegee Institute, investigated primarily for peonage, but their full report, which was never published, later came to include all conditions affecting black refugees.

Thomas M. Campbell, a member of Moton's commission and an extension agent for the Department of Agri-

106

Panther Burn, M

culture, explained how the planters guaranteed that the indebted tenants would remain in the area. Once in the camp, the refugee had to register, "and then he cannot get out unless some outside person makes application for his release with the promise of giving him a home and seeing that he is not a Public Charity Ward. The Labor Agents have not access to the Camps and the Planters have, hence they are able to offer homes to many of our people in the Delta and on the Plantation from which they came." As Cora Lee Campbell remembered it, she did not particularly want to return to Scott, but she did not have anywhere else to go. Because indebtedness was a way of life, most tenants willingly returned to the farms from which they came; the only alternative was to be signed up by a labor agent from an-

The spring planting was due to start, but in some cases refugees were forced to spend several months waiting for the water to leave the fertile land. These were refugees standing outside what looks to be a general store in Panther Burn, Mississippi. (Illinois Central Gulf Railroad)

"The whole question seems to have been whether guards were stationed there to keep the refugees in or to keep the public out," the Colored Advisory Commission reported. A guard checking a woman's tag as she calmly smokes her pipe. (U.S. Signal Corps, in Hoover Library, Album 5-00108)

other agricultural area or from the North, but those agents were forbidden to enter the camps.

Planters' abhorrence of labor agents was a long-standing tradition in the South. Even before the great migration of blacks started in 1916, such agents had been scorned. The white people of Yazoo City, Mississippi, made no secret of their distaste for the agents, or of how they would be treated if caught. "Labor agents will be dealt with on the old time Yazoo plan," announced a vigilante group. "Older citizens do not need assistance in defining the 'Yazoo plan.'" On May 5 the "plan" had almost been effective. "Some alleged labor agents believed to be from an adjoining county of the hills were pursued for a considerable distance by a group of indignant citizens, but the agents 'stepped on the gas' and escaped." The Yazoo plan effectively prevented a free flow of labor during the flood. Throughout the area, planters referred to tenants as "my people."

When members of the Colored Advisory Commission visited the Deeson camp where Cora Lee Campbell was a refugee, they discovered that the behavior of the National Guard evoked the biggest complaint. "The whole question seems to have been whether guards were stationed there to keep the refugees in or to keep the public out," the commissioners reported. They also observed that "in some cases the planters looked upon all outside agencies with disfavor. In other words, the

108

planters were jealous of their Negro labor and did not want any outside interference. However, one planter who did not agree with the majority that soldiers were not needed, said he was glad that they had soldiers at the camp so as to keep the Negroes there, stating further that if the government takes our Negroes and our mules they might just as well take our land."[12]

It was mid-May when the crest of the flood reached Louisiana. With a month's experience in caring for refugees in large camps, the Red Cross moved in with authority, yet it was there that several new problems emerged. For one thing, the refugees seemed very depressed, more so than refugees up the river. Thomas M. Campbell of the Colored Advisory Commission observed this dejection in the Red Cross camp at Baton Rouge on May 17. "I was never so impressed by the intense excitement and fear caused by this terrible catastrophe as I was when I saw these people. They came in by boatloads, eight hundred and a thousand at a time.

The Tallulah Orchestra in front of Red Cross headquarters in Tallulah. (Red Cross)

Despite the worry about the situation back home, life went on, and washing clothes was an essential task in the camps. (Red Cross)

Many were only able to save a few pieces of their wearing apparel and their bed clothing. Men, women, and children were all dazed from the intense strain which they had undergone while fleeing for their lives."[13]

Later Claude A. Barnett, director of the Associated Negro Press, and Jesse O. Thomas, Southern field secretary for the National Urban League, visited camps in Louisiana for the Commission. At Lafayette they found a thriving camp of 21,000 people. The facilities were adequate, they discovered, but the morale of the black refugees was low. They tried to find out why.

"The suddenness of the disaster and the fact that on a number of previous occasions they had been told that water was coming and the water did not come, must have created a feeling closely akin to panic, as information came to them that they must move within a few hours in order to save their lives. The shock of fleeing for their lives and in many instances when water was already in the houses, has left its imprint upon these people. Few of them have gotten back to a normal frame of mind. There is worry about their crops, and there is worry about their hogs, cattle, chickens and the condition of their homes. There are rumors of all sorts that filter into the camps about this house being swept away and about that neighbor having lost all of their mules, etc. To talk to them one gets a conglomerate mass of statements that are depressing. Back of it all, however, there is a feeling of deep gratitude to the Red Cross for having saved their lives. They sit in groups and talk and smile, but one hears no singing or loud laughter. The children romp and play; the mothers look tired and weary and there is, undoubtedly, among the men the feeling of uncertainty as to what will become of them when they leave the refugee camps. They appreciate what is being done for them; they appreciate the friendly attitude of the white officials; they appreciate the kind offices of the colored people who are helping in conducting the affairs of the camp, but they want to get back home. They are curious to know what they will find when they return. One man told us that he carried his chickens, 100 of them, into the attic of his house and left two bushels of corn in the attic with them and then had to climb from the attic window to a ladder and jump on the back of his horse and that the horse swam part of the way to get him to safety."

When Barnett and Thomas left Sicily Island after a surprise inspection there, they boarded a train filled with refugees; water was still over the tracks. "Our train was six hours going eleven miles, crawling through the water at a snail's pace, with frequent stops, the water up to the lower steps of the car, the train in utter darkness the lights having failed, the Jim Crow coach half occupied by whites, and the remainder packed with Negroes some sitting three in a seat, aisles filled with men standing and the noise of the water boiling over the track terrifying one woman until she screamed and put down the window to shut out the sound, with the people refusing to sing because of what seemed to be a sullen resentment at their treatment, it was an experience which will long cling to us."[14]

Two commissioners reported that they rode in a packed train through the flood with "the noise of the water boiling over the track terrifying one woman until she screamed and put down the window to shut out the sound." (Gordon Cotton)

A Nicotine Fit

In the midst of flood relief, Red Cross headquarters faced a weighty problem, one that grew from the peculiar folkways of the rural South. The passing of the bureaucratic buck in the great nicotine crisis of 1927 not only illustrated Delta folkways, but also revealed what an incredible bureaucratic tangle could be made from the sot-weed. Troubled director of disaster relief Henry M. Baker wrote to Red Cross financial director James K. McClintock on May 10, pointing out that "we have been faced in this disaster with a situation wherein we find that tobacco and snuff is just as much a portion of the rations given to negro tenants on these plantations as is molasses and bread." So, using "common sense," Baker agreed to furnish "small supplies of tobacco and snuff unless we were instructed otherwise by you." Herbert Hoover agreed with Baker that tobacco was good for morale.

Yet making things too easy for the unemployed tenants seemed to violate the Protestant Ethic, so on May 19 the Red Cross executives banned manufactured cigarettes but went along with supplying "smoking tobacco, chewing tobacco and snuff only." If tenants smoked, the order implied, the least they could do was roll their own or stuff the tobacco in a pipe. Chewing tobacco and snuff were safe, presumably because no fire was needed to kindle them. Meanwhile, Baker came face to face with the problem of cigars. "So far as I am concerned personally," he wrote on May 27, "I fail to see that cigars can ever be classed as a necessary item for refugees. I do not feel so strongly against cigarettes. However, I would like to see this matter confined strictly to smoking and chewing tobacco exclusive of cigars and

112

One troubled Red Cross worker complained that "lack of tobacco decreases efficiency at least seventy-five per cent," and he urged the National Office to approve tobacco as a part of the rations furnished to the refugees. Catherine Johnson, a former slave, Mary Bankston, and Mary Brown seem content with their life in Natchez. (Red Cross)

At the Panther Burn, Mississippi, depot. The man in the center of the boat was rolling his own cigarette, perhaps with sot-weed furnished by the Red Cross. (Corps of Engineers, Vicksburg, 68-AM-296)

cigarettes." But the Red Cross executives did not understand that tobacco was not just good to the taste, it was imperative for work: "lack of tobacco decreases efficiency at least seventy five percent," explained a local relief worker. Another worker quoted a local planter as saying that if the Red Cross "doesn't get a little bit of tobacco to the negroes down there, they will get restless as they are receiving no pay. He says if he can't get the tobacco to them soon he will have to give them money out of his own pocket and then they will leave camp and go to town, getting into trouble there." By this time Baker saw that he could be in for criticism if the word spread that tobacco was being handed out so freely, so he made the final decision on June 10, telling the local relief staff that tobacco was officially for the old people and that any other kind of disbursement was local responsibility.[15]

"Shall we Gather at the River," was one of the most popular songs during the flood. At St. Peter Catholic Church in New Iberia, Louisiana, the river gathered at the church. (Carroll Studio)

No one pretended that things were easy in the flooded area; conditions left people shocked, dazed, confused, and exhausted. Frederick Simpich, who wrote an article for *National Geographic*, admitted that during three weeks in the flood zone "the only songs I've heard have been camp-meeting hymns like 'Throw out the Life Line' and 'Shall We Gather at the River.' "[16]

Singing hymns, humming the blues, and praying were aspects of normal life that carried over into the refugee camps, helping refugees to accept their fate. Hymnals contained many verses that employed wet metaphors, and while the Catholics and Methodists were sprinkled, Baptists believed in total immersion for salvation. George Moreland, correspondent for the Memphis *Commercial Appeal*, spent the morning of Sunday, May 15, walking by several churches; he commented on the songs chosen for this time of crisis. "The outpourings of praise and supplication in song was particularly noticeable in Alexandria this morning as the worshippers gathered. As a pair of the party passed one edifice there came the strain, 'Throw Out the Life Line, Throw Out the Life Line. Some one is Sinking Today.'

"How suggestive was this when for miles around is almost boundless water.

"On by another church and out on the morning air swelled the chorus of 'Let the lower lights be burning, cast a gleam across the wave, some poor struggling sinking seaman you may rescue, you may save.' "

In Rayville, Louisiana, the flood waters did not stop the congregations of two churches from worshipping. "With the town several feet under water and all business practically suspended, Sunday did not pass without a public religious service. The local pastors arranged for worship on the beautiful river now fronting the Baptist parsonage.

"Six o'clock Sunday evening an immense flotilla bearing crowds of cheerful worshippers assembled on the broad sheet of water for vesper services.

"Dr. W. A. Borum of the Baptist Church and the Rev. Mr. Alford of the Methodist Church conducted devotional exercises. The programme began with 'Shall We Gather at the River.' Several tender prayers were offered.

"Services closed by all singing 'Lord, Plant My Feet on Higher Ground.' "[17]

Turner Catledge heard some refugees in Memphis singing

> Jesus, lover of my soul,
>   Let me to Thy bosom fly.
> While the nearer waters roll,
>   While the tempest still is high.[18]

Preachers of all denominations took it upon themselves to decide whether rain fell upon the just, the unjust, or both. The Reverend Ben Cox of the Central Baptist Church in Memphis went to some length to develop his theme. "Some one says, 'Why the flood?' Adam and Eve started out in a dispensation of innocence. They fell, knew the difference between good and evil,

A church raised its steeple above the flood in Bordelonville, Louisiana. (Paul Coco)

were banished from the Garden, then came the dispensation of conscience. Wonderful developments were made materially and physically, for we are told there were giants in those days. Certainly the eugenists would have been well satisfied. But we read 'And God saw that the wickedness of man was great in the earth.' Does God see now? Does He see corruption in politics, corruption in business? Does He see the inroads of free love? Does He see the petting parties? Does He see the dress of some of our women? God saw and God sent the flood." The Reverend W. P. McLennan of the Seventh Day Adventist Church in Memphis preached that "Such outbursts of satanic wrath as the present flood are harbingers of the coming of Jesus Christ." And Ben T. Bogard wrote in *The Baptist and Commoner* that the flood "should bring us to our knees before God. It is God's alarm clock going off to warn us of danger."

But not all religious leaders thought in apocalyptic terms. The Very Reverend Israel H. Noe preached a sermon of moderation to his congregation at St. Mary's Cathedral in Memphis. "There are many people in Memphis who believe that the recent floods have been sent by God upon the people of this territory because of some great sin they have committed, although God's Bible tells us plainly that He makes the rain to fall upon the just and the unjust."[19]

Nearly every relief camp set up services for the refugees, and these served as yet another contact with the routine of life that existed in normal times. They were especially important in time of crisis. Evangelical preachers, like home demonstration agents, treated the massive relief camps as missionary fields ripe unto the harvest. Some circulated throughout the camps praying and handing out literature. While their activities were well intentioned, they sometimes brought sharp criticism. Jules B. Jeannard, Bishop of Lafayette, Louisiana, did not mind the Protestants holding regular services, but on May 27, in a letter to the editor of the Lafayette *Daily Advertiser*, he complained of preachers who were proselytizing. He had visited a hundred Catholic families in the camp, he wrote, "and was grieved and pained to learn that every one of them had been approached by the preachers who left their literature in their tents. A dear old lady weepingly told me that their only comfort and consolation in this dark hour was their Catholic faith and, having lost everything else, it did not seem right that attempts should now be made to rob them of this."

What Father Jeannard resented, he explained in another letter, was that people from what amounted to a different culture had invaded his parish. French Louisiana was different, and nearly all Red Cross workers and other observers from outside Louisiana were immediately impressed by the French-speaking Cajuns. Turner Catledge, ever on hand to comment and inform his readers about new developments in the flood, observed that "The refugees down in here are the strangest of all refugees. They are mostly of French descent, extremely timid and even resentful at times. They emphatically resent being photographed, voicing their disapproval in a conglomeration of broken French and English. They are deeply sentimental and the flood took on a sorrowful aspect around Mansura today when these Arcadians began to mourn for their homes now under the muddy flood water from the rising river."[20]

Even the most elemental aspects of relief were different in Louisiana, for in custom, religion, and diet the French influence was deeply implanted. Maude Cham-

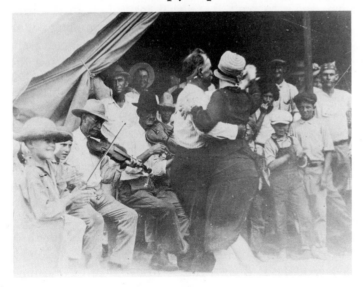

Fiddling and grinning at the Lafayette, Louisiana, refugee camp. Cajun culture, observers agreed, was both distinct and attractive. (Red Cross)

bers, a nutrition nurse, took a common-sense approach when she set up the meals for the Baton Rouge camp. Arguing that "the path to good nutrition should be paved with psychology," she talked with many refugees. "Going to another group I am greeted with Cajun jabber with a sprinkling of English. I take Mrs. Gautheier's picture. Eighty-three years old and can't speak English. I can't speak French. In our separate languages though, from day to day, we hold long conversations. Her eyes are kindly, behind the new spectacles. She had lost those in her hasty retreat when the levee broke. 'Meat— I have to have meat,' she entreats. 'Do you like cornbread or bread?' a 'feeler' in my meal planning scheme. 'My children and me, we eat cornbread and syrup.' 'Cafe au lait?' 'Oui, and syrup.' There you have the good habit of the main of one poor Bayou des Glaises family. Do I intend to feed them just what they've been accustomed to? I do not. They would like gumbo with rice and coffee every day. I give them gumbo once a week— not the expensive chicken gumbo a New Yorker gloats over in Antione's but—weine gumbo. 'Cafe au lait' for the children is an universal custom. That must be stopped."

Yet Maude Chambers discovered that Cajun customs and good manners were winning her over. "Among the eligible foods, first, last and all the time, coffee. You may come to scoff this social institution in southern Louisiana, but you become a convert if you don't watch out." But her feeling for the French people went deeper. "The most docile, the most courteous but the most individualistic people on the face of the globe— 'The Cajuns.'" The people were appreciative, she reported. "They pat you in passing or even more—these women. After all, human nature is the same whether its in Bayou des Glaises, Louisiana, or Long Island, New York. We love, we hate—and, how we do eat!"[21]

It was inevitable that camp life would produce urban problems in tent cities occupied by such recent residents of farm areas. So many people packed so tightly, waiting impatiently to return to they knew not what, set the stage for problems. For some inexplicable reason officials of the Red Cross failed to heed earlier warnings about the spread of venereal disease until the situation reached a crisis. Dr. Valeria H. Parker explained the problem to Red Cross Director of Medical and Health Activities Dr. William R. Redden. "Acute gonococcus infections among soldier-guards; promiscuity between guards and girls in both white and colored camps; intimacy between young people in refugee camps; use of a refugee tent for purposes of prostitution by a married woman whose husband secured the customers; expulsion of five unattached girls sexually promiscuous and suspected as sources of venereal infection; disappearance of a young unmarried woman who miscarried in camp hospital. The latter was assisted in making her escape by soldier-guards who brought her clothing to the hospital. It was learned that the girl, who was a student nurse, had gone to an aunt in the State of Ohio. The girls who were ejected from camp were sent to another State, but no notification of their diseased condition or moral delinquency was made to any social or health Agency in the State to which they were sent." Parker demanded that at least policewomen be employed in the camps.

Eventually the Red Cross hierarchy responded to the problem by sending in a team from the American Social Hygiene Association of New York. Among others, Dr. Albert J. Read and Margaret Wells Wood toured the camps that remained open in early June. They gave lectures on social hygiene; in other words, they explained the consequences of promiscuity and venereal disease. As Margaret Wood explained in a report to Valeria Parker, "We frankly discussed types of dancing, loitering around men (soldiers especially) and the end results of 'pick-ups,' first indiscretions etc., using as a very telling illustration the first leaks in the levee that later resulted in the uncontrollable crevasse. The girls were delightfully frank, interested and appreciative."[22]

In most cases the social hygiene people were accepted as professionals who had something important to say and could help control social problems in the camps. Dr. Albert Read arrived in Lafayette and talked to Captain F. B. Putney, who was in charge of the camp there. "Glad you people have arrived," Read quoted Putney as

A street of water in Moreauville, Louisiana. (Paul Coco)

responding, "we need you. I have 35 men now arrested for indecency and at work on the rock pile. I ran one man out of town at point of bayonet. Some of the offenders are refugees and some are town men who have been arrested for invading restricted area. Two women from New Orleans got in as refugees and started business the second day after being assigned a tent. I gave them 24 hrs. to get out of town, as I had no jail suitable for women." The fact that Putney was arresting people and putting them to work on the rock pile alarmed DeWitt Smith, a Red Cross official, and he wrote in the margin of Read's report, "If Putney is correctly quoted I think you may want to caution him."[23]

In some cases, however, Read and Wood were carefully questioned before being allowed to speak. Read quoted one Catholic priest as stating bluntly, "We hope this is not anything on birth control." The most bizarre objection to the lectures came from Adjutant General L. A. Toombs of Louisiana. Dr. Read could not hide his incredulity as he reported that Toombs objected "on the ground that immorality had been reported and the National Guard criticized. He said he allowed no one but himself to criticize the guard. He said the statement of a negro at Opelousas was not reliable, that Northern people did not understand conditions in the South. As his word was supreme, no lecture was given to the National Guard of Louisiana and Alabama at Camp Beauregard."[24]

In addition to their lectures, Read, Wood, and other workers did quite a bit of investigating into the social life of Louisiana and Mississippi. "The boys around here are 'free' (promiscuous) with girls," Read quoted a Louisiana camp employee as explaining to him, "but they wash theirselves with 'white mule' (corn whiskey) and never or most never get any disease." Another employee, evidently impatient with the young folks, dismissed them as "a bad lot of children, they are like wild beasts, you can't do anything with them." A priest from Bordelonville told Read, "Never hear of sodomy here, but many illegitimacies. Relatives take the child and then compel the couple to marry. They are not happy unions. Think parent's laxness is at fault." Two couples

120

did not have to wait long for matrimony, Parker reported. "The morning before my arrival, two young women who had been absent from their tents all night were reported by their families. The two young men involved were brought to the Dispensary Tent for physical examination (such examination is required by law in Louisiana before marriage). The two couples were married immediately afterward."[25]

To the puritanical Red Cross, any sexual promiscuity was dreadful and had to be hushed up. But to the people who dealt with social hygiene, it was all in a day's work to talk about sex education. To leave the story of the New Yorkers without recording their impression of the South would be to miss the main thrust of their work, for most of all they were concerned with improving people's lives. Margaret Wells Wood noted that the people in Louisiana had admirable values. "Having had all material possessions swept away by the flood, they keenly realize that family unity and social well-being, the greatest possession, is still in their keeping. They also see that social disaster is far more to be dreaded than loss of cattle, rugs, dearly beloved sewing machine or photograph." She had a tremendous empathy with the friendly Cajun women. "Poor, starved, hungry, lonely women—they welcome friendly advances," she reported. "The great difficulty that these women face in the training of their children is that they, the mothers, belong to a different order that knows nothing of the movie, the modern dance, rouge and lisptick and the accompanying freedom and equality of women."[26]

Life in the South had not been easy for Margaret Wood. Unlike dietitian Maude Chambers, Wood did not take to Cajun food. "Personally, I was glad to leave Opelousas for the living conditions were terrible! Greasy food that was uneatable, so I survived on ice-cream and chocolate malted milks at the Drug Store." The food aside, it had been a moving experience for her. "One leaves groups reached in these camps feeling the universality of womanhood, appreciating keenly the fine native instincts and gracious bearing of those of French descent, and deploring the lack of opportunity most of the adults have had to build upon these fine natural

121

Above all else, refugees sought to keep their families intact and healthy. The Red Cross faced most problems with candor and efficiency, but when a venereal epidemic broke out, they were reluctant to admit that it was serious. This family enjoyed rations and togetherness. (Red Cross)

endowments." She said the only hope for developing these fine talents would be a better school system.[27]

Long after the water receded, Dr. William R. Redden was trying to minimize the sexual problems that sprang up in the camps. Alarmed that some of the problems might be publicized, he quibbled with Dr. Valeria H. Parker over her statement that the Red Cross had become aware of the crisis only late in the game. He warned her that "it is not customary for the Red Cross Disaster Relief operations to publish articles of any kind which will discredit the recipients of Red Cross relief no matter of how much importance such reports might seem to have from a general public health point of view."[28]

The Red Cross hierarchy tried to keep the publicity lid on all of the major problems of relief. Though their task had been performed admirably, even nobly in most cases, the organization feared that publicizing the peonage, the high number of drownings, and the venereal disease epidemics would dry up the funds that the flood had initiated. Yet the Red Cross treasury was filled with money for rehabilitation, and in the autumn Red Cross officials actually considered diverting some of the relief money into construction of levees. Congress had not been called into special session to deal with flood control, and the local levee boards were bankrupt, so the sagging levees were an open invitation for the high water of 1928 to rush back across the land. Neither Congress nor President Coolidge furnished leadership for flood control or relief; thus the Red Cross probably assumed that it was the only organization that would respond to the levee problem.

Margaret Wood summarized the difficulties facing the refugees, and at the same time she condemned the economic and social customs of the South. "A people, worn out by the ravages of tuberculosis, pellagra, and venereal diseases, with little resistance due to unsanitary living conditions and lack of education, an economic debit instead of an asset, could be thereby restored to rightful and healthful standards of living in this so-termed 'land of opportunity' and society in general would be the gainer. A Revolutionary step has been taken in this disaster when human values were placed first and when like programs of their betterment were extended to all people no matter what color the skin chanced to be."[29]

5

reconstruction

"They go with the spirit of the Southerners of reconstruction days to build again anew," reported the Lafayette *Daily Advertiser* on June 18, 1927. Indeed, Sherman's march had not wreaked as much havoc as the flood. For refugees who left their houses buried beneath a yellow sea, returning home meant anxiety, not joy. Those who were luckiest only had to clean out the mud; the less fortunate did not have any homes to return to, for out of the 162,000 that were flooded, nearly 9000 homes were totally destroyed.

Margaret Wells Wood moved northward after giving social hygiene lectures in Louisiana; she went to Mississippi as the people were returning to their homes, and recorded the scene. "And everywhere a vast expanse of drab brown, barren earth—emerging from mucky fields

Refugees from the Bayou des Glaises returning home after the flood. (Red Cross)

Nearly 9000 homes were destroyed by the flood, including this one in the Mississippi Delta. (William A. Percy Library)

A church completely wrecked by wind and water. "The rain descended, and the floods came, and the winds blew, and beat upon that house; and it fell; and great was the fall of it." Matthew 7:27. (William A. Percy Library)

from which the miles and miles of water are slowly receding. High on cabin, barn, telegraph pole and tree can be seen the dark brown line that marks the height to which the waters reached. Little wonder that all shake their heads at the thought of the home-going, knowing full well the devastation wrought by the flood waters, the endless labor to retrieve losses, the long period without funds, and the isolation resulting from the loss of the dearly beloved old Ford or the faithful mules, that used to carry them over roads and bridges now washed away.

"The thought of the return to the plantation was not a happy one. Devastated cabins, insufficient furnishing, losses of treasured beds or cattle or crops, the long remembrance of other scores still unsettled, of overcharges for supplies bought under compulsion at the

Anna Bowie, Minna Bell Chandler, and M. T. Young posing in front of the Sparta Gin in Dockport, Louisiana. Such scenes prompted one observer to comment on the psychological marks on the people, writing that "they are deeply seared scars upon the face of the fair land, and more deeply still upon the hearts, and the minds, and the hopes, and the very futures of the young and the old." (Corps of Engineers, Vicksburg, 67-AM-137)

"The odor was terrible," remembered one woman who lived in Greenville. No doubt these fish rotting in the sun added to the smell. (Mississippi Levee Commissioners)

plantation store, these and other gloomy thoughts surged through their simple minds. 'Plantation blues' of an order not traditionally associated with these humble black folks were everywhere apparent. And on every hand one hears from white lips, 'There is no way out.' "[1]

The flood destroyed homes and property, but it also left its mark on the people. "I drove to Greenville today," F. H. Deverto wrote in July to Dr. John McMullen of the U.S. Public Health Service. "I took my family with me. The water has all gone. But, its marks are left. They are not marks, but rather are they scars like war makes upon a countryside. And they are deeply seared scars upon the face of the fair land, and more deeply still upon the hearts, and the minds, and the hopes, and the very futures of the young and the old. They are not scars of an event, but rather are they the scars that mark an epoch in the life of this section. A bravado may be attempted to throw off that feeling that comes to the mind and is visible in the eye of all who have lived through it to face this awful ruin and waste in property and in human toll; but it shall require long years of unremitting toil and sleepless nights to make the land and the debts and the homes and the schools and the education of the young repay the needed labor and effort before us all."[2]

Mrs. E. J. Smith, Virginia Montgomery Pullen's sister, had been teaching school in southern Mississippi. She

128

went to Greenville to help her father clean up before the remainder of the family returned. "Daddy had raked the mud out of the house and gotten most of the rattle-snakes out," she remembers. "The smell was there. It smelled terrible." E. E. Bass, a Greenville schoolteacher, agreed. "As soon as the water went out of the back rooms we cleaned the mud out and scoured. The odor was terrible." His sister had continual fights with cray-fish in the rooms where water remained, while frogs, cockroaches, and water bugs made themselves at home. After three months at the Deeson camp, Cora Lee Campbell reluctantly returned to Scott. "Snakes in the houses and all like that, and the things we'd done left in the house, they wasn't fittin for nothing," she remembered.[3]

Clarendon, Arkansas, was probably typical. "The stores are wrecked and their perishable stock is rot-ting in the streets," reported the Memphis *Commercial Appeal* on May 6. "The stench in Clarendon is unbear-able. Mud and slime fill the streets. A carload of lime for disinfecting purposes is to arrive tomorrow. The spirit of the people, which has been good until today, suffered a noticeable letdown as the full extent of their calamity dawned upon them. Some of the residences have been cleaned out and the wrecked furniture thrown into the streets."[4]

Effects of the high water in Greenville. (Mississippi Levee Commissioners, Mrs. Horace Polk Collection)

The Tom Newton Plantation

The Tom Newton plantation rested on the south bank of the Arkansas River, ten miles northwest of Little Rock, and prior to the flood it contained 600 acres, 550 of them planted in crops. Newton had the usual plantation appointments: a home, commissary, barn, some smaller buildings, and seventeen tenant houses. Besides the mules, hogs, and cattle, there was a Case thresher, a tractor, and even a Delco light plant and indoor plumbing for the "central plantation buildings."

On July 18, 1927, in the aftermath of the flood, three agricultural experts from the University of Arkansas surveyed the plantation, in an attempt to determine if the damage could be repaired and the soil restored. They had with them M. R. Beatty, a staff photographer from the Arkansas *Gazette*. The report and the accompanying photographs give an account of what the investigators said was "representative of a number of plantations in the flooded area."

"There is no levee protection and the flood waters covered the entire plantation," the report explained.

A building on the Tom Newton plantation in Arkansas. As the Agriculture Department observers noted, some of the buildings "are in holes that have been washed out as the waters swirled around them." (Hoover Library)

"Forty acres of land caved into the river; 100 acres were badly washed, causing holes and gullies; 450 acres were covered with sand, most of which seemed to be from 6 to 18 inches deep, though there are sand drifts which are much deeper. Seventy-five acres of the plantation have been made entirely untillable." Instead of the usual twelve tenants tilling the land, there were only five, and only one of them lived on the place.

"The loss of plantation buildings," the report continued, "such as the barn, potato house, tool shed, and other outbuildings, is almost complete, as there is very little material in these buildings which can be salvaged without considerable expense. These buildings are in holes that have been washed out as the waters swirled around them. Of the 17 tenant houses that were on the plantation before the flood, there is only one left stand-

Another building on the Newton plantation. Sand washed over the plantation, making the soil unfit for raising cash crops. (Hoover Library)

ing. These tenant houses have been carried away and there is no salvage for them."

Nearly all of the implements had been destroyed. "A Case thresher is at the bottom of a large hole washed out by the flood and appears to be a complete loss. A tractor is under the potato house in another hole and is apparently ruined."

Six mules, 15 head of cattle, and 25 hogs had drowned in the swift current. The waters had also taken 40 tons of hay, 1200 bushels of corn, 30 tons of cottonseed, and 75 bushels of oats.

Despite what looked like complete ruin, the University of Arkansas investigators argued that it was "entirely feasible and practical" to restore the land to productivity. "The process of restoring normal productivity of the soil will necessarily have to be extended over a period of years," they observed, and the task would not be easy. The land had first to be leveled out by plowing and dragging soil to fill in the low places. Then they outlined a six-point plan of crop-rotation plowing, and a wise selection of crops for the different soil types. "While a large portion of the farm which formerly consisted of clay soil has been converted into a sandy soil," they reasoned, "it is practical to make it again productive by growing crops which will add organic matter to the soil."

If the heavily damaged Newton plantation had potential for restoration, there was hope for other damaged plantations along the Arkansas River. The team of investigators noted finally that the process of reclamation would be lengthy and expensive.

But they did not mention the possibility that the river could again flood the Newton plantation and all the others along the river.[5]

The Red Cross supplied needed articles of furniture, food, clothing, and seed; the agency also provided repairs for 22,000 homes, feed for 60,000 animals, and replaced 1600 farm implements. In order to encourage sanitation, in each county seat the Red Cross sponsored a model outdoor toilet for the rural people to inspect. The Red Cross also gave away tons of yeast to combat pellagra and established a follow-up health campaign.

In the early days of the flood the Red Cross had high expectations for reconstruction. On May 28 Herbert Hoover outlined his plans in a national radio address. "I have used the term 'reconstruction' advisedly," he explained, "because I should like to turn the implications of that term in the relations of the North to the South into a term of sympathy instead of a term of hate."[6] Yet the Red Cross did not provide adequate relief for all refugees, and Congress did not meet in special session to consider additional relief legislation.

Hoover did, however, set up credit organizations to aid people crushed by the disaster. In Mississippi, Arkansas, and Louisiana leading bankers and businessmen, aided by bankers outside the South, set up temporary credit corporations to meet the crisis. Some leaders were reluctant to extend credit, and Hoover occasionally resorted to surprising means to implement his plan.

"Mr. Hoover came back to Memphis determined to organize a local corporation to make low-interest loans to land-owners, and sharecroppers through their land-owners, on a strictly business basis," Turner Catledge remembered. "The plan had no suggestion of Federal subsidies of any kind. He called a meeting at the Peabody Hotel of a group of leading citizens. One of these was a very good contact of mine, a tough banker named

L. C. Speers, in the New York *Times,* gave a description of this scene. "With a suddenness that is startling the flood zone comes into view. The machine slows down and creeps over tortuous ruts and deep gulches. Standing out with startling distinction is the wreck of a two-story mansion. On 'Crevasse Day' morning it was the home of Dr. Andrew Fox, and was the most imposing structure for miles around. Today the kitchen is where the living room was and the cupola is tilted to an angle of 45 degrees.

"In front of the mansion is the first of the crevasses, revealing the force of the water that poured through the gap. For acres the ground is toothed and ripped open, in places the erosion being ten and fifteen feet deep. A hundred yards further on is another big house even more of a wreck than the Fox house, while the wreckage of small farmhouses that collapsed is everywhere to be seen." (Louisiana Dept. of Public Works)

Brinkley Snowden, who was vice president and practically owner of the Bank of Commerce. Snowden's family owned vast acres of land across the river in Arkansas. . . .

"Mr. Snowden told me, 'This man Hoover is awfully tough. He told us we'd have to get up five million dollars by the time his train leaves at five o'clock this afternoon. We've never raised or committed money like that before, not even during the yellow fever crisis.' I said, 'Well, Mr. Snowden, what are you going to do?' He said, 'We're going to get it up, because he told us if we didn't get up the necessary funds to resettle the refu-

The caprice of the flood makes this scene appear almost as a before and after sequence, but it is all after. With the land so eroded, it is no wonder that farmers asked for tax breaks for 1927. (Louisiana Dept. of Public Works)

gees, he'd start moving our niggers out of here to the north, this very night.' And they got up the five million dollars."

Ever mindful of the economic and political consequences of a series of bank failures in the South, Hoover explained his motivations more clearly in a telegram to Louis Pearson, President of the Chamber of Commerce of the United States. "We cannot afford nationally to have a business or financial prairie fire starting from here after the flood."[7]

Despite Hoover's efforts, plantation owners had problems. O. J. Hill wrote to Governor John E. Martineau of Arkansas complaining of impending tax bills and reflecting on the economic gloom of the area. "I own a 3000 acre plantation in Poinsett Co. near Truman," he began. "It has been under water from the St. Francis river. The water is receding but continuous rains have made it impossible to plant any cotton & it looks now as if we could not plant corn & hay.

"I have 60 families on the place which I have borrowed money to maintain.

"My state & county taxes are due.

"Heretofore I have been able to borrow money to pay taxes & make a crop when needed.

"In the face of these conditions I can't do it. What are we flooded farmers to do?

Louisianans trying to put their farm back together after the flood. (Louisiana Dept. of Public Works)

"Should we have a 25% penalty put on us for non-payment in times like these?

"Could you not very consistently issue a proclamation calling off all penalties on taxes for one year to all whose land has been so wet they could not plant crops so far? We are up against a fearful situation and it seems to me this is one way you can help save the farmers, over-flowed, from bankruptcy."[8]

What O. J. Hill had found at his plantation was typical of the lands throughout the flood area. E. T. Cashion of Eudora, Arkansas, gave a general description of his county to Governor Martineau. "There are at least three hundred *families* in this county who had arranged to farm but they will not now be able to do so because of the fact that water is still in their homes; then too many planters will be unable to go ahead with tenants because many could barely make arrangements for funds with which to feed the families and the live stock. Now fences are gone, houses are destroyed or seriously damaged and the land owner has not the means nor the credit with which to repair these damages. He is therefore compelled to turn many of his tenants loose to shift for themselves. So far those farm families are being fed by the Red Cross. But this cant continue indefinitely. There are no industries here to absorb this labor; the community is unable to cope with the situation.

"Then there is the town population. Merchants and business men are cutting expenses; and many people who have had satisfactory employment in the past are

136

now idle. They had set aside nothing for emergencies and have no way to turn to employment. Many could not raise railroad fare to the next station from their homes. Ninety-nine per cent of them are willing and anxious to find something to do so that they can continue to support their families.

"The picture is rather dark, yet facts must be faced by level-headed men and women. When men become physically ill, and without funds, there are many institutions and doctors who will do all in their power to restore them to health; when those same men are well in body but down and out financially something can surely be done to again make them self sustaining."[9]

Although the National Red Cross attempted to rehabilitate flood victims, local customs or simple indifference often undid the organization's best efforts. Mrs. Bird Tatum, a home demonstration agent from St. Francis County, Arkansas, reported some of her frustrations. "As the refugees went back into the bottoms, I took the Red Cross Nurse with me and helped her with vaccinations and the health program in general. The food question was never omitted. The State Board of Health sent two doctors to our county to work on a program of rural sanitation. I went with them as often as I could to night meetings, too.

"I talked with our local chairmen of the Red Cross on several occasions about needs, etc. They were always nice, but never acted upon any suggestion.

This structure stopped just short of the road, but it would take another flood to float it back to its foundations. (Louisiana Dept. of Public Works)

The caption on this photo read: "What remains of a plantation site. In the background the hole in which the man is standing was washed beneath the farm house before it was finally wrecked and washed away. The hole in the foreground in which the lady stands was washed beneath the barn before it was carried away by the waters. These holes are between 15 and 25 feet deep." (William A. Percy Library)

"Cotton, cotton was all they wanted and could see, so I kept busy with my regular program. Rehabilitation work begun, I thought they would grant me some things. I was awfully disappointed. Mr. Evans who is the Red Cross Director is heartily in sympathy with the Extension Program of work and is trying to open their eyes."[10]

The inner workings of the agricultural system were not apparent to all who toured the flood area, but one could hardly miss the heavy hand of destruction that lay over the land. Frank M. Heath, who traveled through the flood area in the summer, was struck by the distortion of the landscape. Near Winnsboro, Louisiana, he reported that "the scene is one of desolation. Houses are washed off their foundation—usually piers or piles, and are anywhere from a few hundred feet away in any imaginable angle, out of plumb in all degrees, just as the flood left them. Families are living in some of these. Other houses, they tell me, are fifty miles down stream. Some of those we see come from nobody knows where, like a stray cat. Ownership seems to have been lost sight of. They stand, sit, or lean there in the mud or perhaps partly under water, in a state of utter indifference."[11]

During the summer, as the water drained to the Gulf, Robert R. Moton, chairman of the Colored Advisory Commission, held off making public the most dismal parts of his investigation. When Hoover read the reports that supported complaints of peonage and discrimination, he urged Moton that the best course was to act privately and not publicize the situation. Hoover assured Moton that the Red Cross would push a giant rehabilitation effort to change the agricultural arrangements along the river. An excited Moton wrote to Hoover on June 13, revealing his dream of making the Delta of Mississippi and other flooded areas a better place for black workers. "We were interested in a song that these people sang in the levee camps—that the flood had washed away the old account. They felt that

Charles G. Dawes, Vice President of the United States, was sleeping in the car just behind the one hanging over the bayou. The engine plunged into forty-two feet of water killing engineer Sam Jones; another engineer and the fireman escaped with slight injuries. Dawes was returning from addressing the American Legion Convention at Greenville when, just after midnight on July 28, the engine crashed through the flood-weakened trestle one half mile south of Head, Mississippi. Dawes slept through the accident and the ensuing excitement. The fact that the train was creeping along at five miles an hour saved the Vice President and the other passengers from catastrophe. The next day as 2000 people crowded around, diver J. A. Leahy tried five times before finally bringing up Jones's body from the water. (Corps of Engineers, Vicksburg, 67-AM-181)

139

the flood had emancipated them from a condition of peonage."[12] Yet Hoover had overestimated his power in the South. He was unable to set up the kind of rehabilitation that he had promised Moton.

Indeed, as autumn came and the weather chilled, Moton became alarmed that even basic human needs would not be met by the Red Cross. Black investigators attempted to find those families who were most in need, and some of the reports reveal the miserable conditions following the flood.

Jerushia P. Griffin traveled through Louisiana to visit back-country families and made his report to Dr. J. S. Clark, president of Southern University, who in turn forwarded the material to Moton. "Frances and Robert Cooper were visited," Griffin wrote on November 4. "They were sleeping on the floor, a pair of rusted springs and a mattress constituting their bed. The broad fire place held her pots and skillets where she was trying to prepare her working husband's dinner. 1 pair of springs, 1 bed, 1 stove, and a pair of shoes were recommended for this family." On November 22 he visited the home of six people. "Etta Higgins had 2 children to get burned up in August, and one run over by an automobile two days prior to my visit. I recommended clothing and shoes for the remaining four."[13]

By late fall the opportunity to gain national support for reform in the South had disappeared; people quickly forgot about the flood and its victims. Moton, however, writing up his report on a November tour of the flood area, refused to ease his statements about the harsh conditions. His draft report outraged and frightened the Red Cross and Hoover. On December 16 Hoover wrote Moton an indignant reply, reminding him of the rescue and relief role of the Red Cross; the letter revealed as well Hoover's continued belief that blacks were better off than ever. "In the large sense, we must remember that 400,000 colored people were rescued from the flood, with the loss of scarcely two lives after our organization was initiated; that the present condition among them, as reported by the health units established through the aid of the Rockefeller Foundation, is better than before the flood, and this is borne out by all statistical evidence as to illness and death." To Hoover's mind, such reports as those of Jerushia Griffin were inconsequential.

James Fieser described Moton's reception at Hoover's office a few days later. "Mr. Hoover says he 'laid Dr. Moton out' when he was in his office yesterday morning and told him in decency the report should at the outset have recited some of the fine things the Red Cross has done and that after a paragraph of that he would not have cared what else they said. Mr. Moton promised to do just that and have the report recast." So Moton recast the report, and when it appeared it contained nothing derogatory about the Red Cross, and it also did not mention any of the crucial problems that blacks faced in the South. Moton's capitulation illustrated that a black man, whether a refugee in a camp along the river or the president of a college, dared not challenge the whites who controlled him.[14]

Modern Inventions and Enterprising Daring

It seemed that every person who had ever watched a drainage ditch overflow had a plan to control the Mississippi River, for hundreds of would-be engineers dusted off their schemes and sent them to Herbert Hoover. The proposed solutions varied from the thoughtless to the bizarre; nearly all novice engineers visualized the Father of Waters as having the same constancy of width and depth as the Erie Canal. A. C. Jones of Laramie, Wyoming, set the tone when he asserted that if "the Chinese using primitive methods of two thousand years ago, could build a wall 2,550 miles long as a defense against invaders, we, with our modern inventions and enterprising daring, can at least attempt to emulate them."

Some students of the river did not see any need for inventions or daring. "The recent flood which has done such a great damage in the south would not have happened," announced ecology-minded J. McClean of Saranac Lake, New York, "if the states which drain into this great river had their woodland streams stocked with beavers." Sidney V. Lowell of Brooklyn, on the other hand, saw a profound natural imbalance creeping over the entire globe. "When in Europe this year," he confided, "I found a deep seated conviction that the extreme use of electricity in recent years has affected the

Story B. Ladd's Persian solution to floods in the Mississippi Valley. When the water rose, people would simply go to the raft, tie it to a mooring mast, and the raft would float above the flood. (Hoover Library)

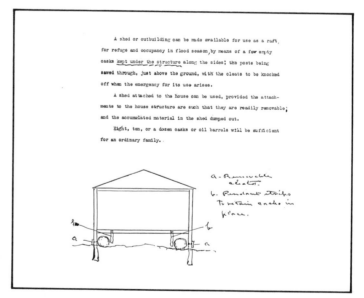

A shed or outbuilding can be made available for use as a raft, for refuge and occupancy in flood season, by means of a few empty casks kept under the structure along the sides; the posts being sawed through, just above the ground, with the cleats to be knocked off when the emergency for its use arises.

A shed attached to the house can be used, provided the attachments to the house structure are such that they are readily removable; and the accumulated material in the shed dumped out.

Eight, ten, or a dozen casks or oil barrels will be sufficient for an ordinary family.

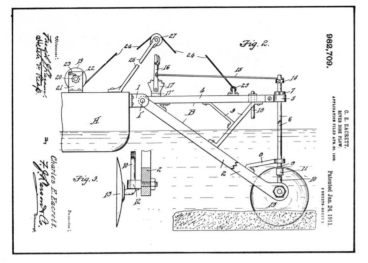

atmosphere so as to bring excessive rain and consequent floods."

Story B. Ladd of Washington, D.C., who had no doubt spent many a day roaming through the Smithsonian Institution, urged that a Persian custom be adopted along the Mississippi and its tributaries. Persians, he informed Hoover, had constructed rafts with inflated skins for crossing the river "in their biannual migrations between summer and winter grounds." All a plantation needed, Ladd suggested, was a mooring mast and a raft with a tent or shed on it. When the water rose, the people would simply go to the raft, tie it to the mast, and the raft would float above the flood. To make sure that Hoover understood, he included a sketch of the raft.

Several people, apparently thinking that the river bottom was like a flat, water-covered field, suggested that a disk plow could be installed on a steamboat' or tug. This device would deepen the channel as the disk turned the mud and the water pushed it to sea. As C. E. Eacrett of Malvern, Iowa, explained it, "These Disk Plows fitted and attached to a steamboat, to plow up the bottom of the rivers, for nine or ten months of the year, thus helping the river current to deepen the channel." Eacrett had a patent on such a plow, and informed Hoover that "the patent No 982.709. is for sale. How much am I offered?" Eacrett had failed to consider the river's varying depths, its snags, and the volume of water and mud that already filled it. Such a plow, had it ever touched bottom, would have barely tickled the riverbed. The idea had staying power, though, and Frank Fredeen of Minneapolis appeared before a congressional committee in January 1928, confident that his plowing plan would work. Though he lacked a patent, Fredeen had tested his plow in Washington's Rock Creek; he was confident that the current would move the silt downstream, deepening the channel. The committee chairman appointed two reluctant members to investigate the feasibility of Fredeen's plows. The record does not reveal the results.

A Navy man sought to put the fleet to work and suggested that Hoover "take these destroyers at San Diego, Calif. Head them up stream full speed with ankers enough to hold theme in place stern ankers." He believed that the propellers would push the water rapidly into the Gulf of Mexcio before it had a chance to break a levee.

A budding St. Paul engineer thought flood control was simply a matter of plumbing. "Why can we not handle the Mississippi problem as we do the surplus water in our city streets? We have thousands of miles of sewers costing millions, not only for sewerage but to carry off the surplus water." He suggested that a sewer pipe be built along the levee to carry off excess water. After all, "Oil is transported many thousand miles in this way."

Such sewer pipes would not be needed if people in the Upper Valley would carry out an ingenious plan reported in the Monroe, Louisiana, *News-Star:* collect the rain water in barrels as it came off the houses and dump it out when the river was low. Evidently the originator of this plan thought that all rain fell not on the just and the unjust, but on the housetops.

Some of the plans were so complicated that they grew beyond the comprehension of even the inventors. Elmer Robinson of Modesto, California, sent a diagram of a complex machine that would keep all the rivers "at certain stage, without use of Electricity or Steam *water only.*" The device, which resembled a commode, would

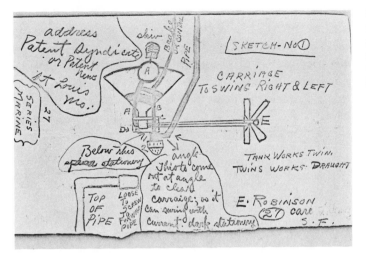

Elmer Robinson's invention would keep the river "at certain stage, without use of Electricity or Steam water only." (Hoover Library)

discharge water into a drainage ditch when the river reached a certain level.

I. E. Officer of Freeport, Illinois, invented a machine so intricate that its explanation evoked the mysticism of the Book of Revelation. It contained "a series of elevators built on a Barge, these elevators would consist of six units of elevators. Each unit being driven seperate from other unites and consisting of ten sets of cups, carried on ten set of double sprock chains." Officer wanted to dredge out the sand from the center of the river and allow the cups to dump it 600 to 1000 feet from the main channel. The only shortcoming, he theorized, would occur if the sand would "drift back again to the center, but when you have the channel opened up straight it will be an easy matter to run this machine down over the same ground again." It didn't appear that it would be an easy matter to run the machine at all, but Officer had already received encouragement from his Congressman.

"A Citizen," in a more easily grasped plan, suggested "a series of large iron pipes, to be about say eight feet in diameter, and laid from the bed of the Mississippi River and extending to the arid lands of the far west." A drawing was enclosed.

Vladimir Skrivauck suggested his method in a ten-page paper, "Take the Kinks out of Mississippi!" This was later done.

"A Citizen" thought that pipelines should carry the water to the dry areas of the West. (Hoover Library)

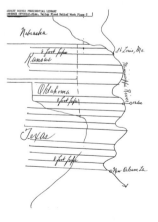

145

The frenzy was international. From Bucharest, Rumania, the M.M.D. Vituac Company wrote that "without the outlay of a single dollar, it is possible to carry out the totality of protective works against all inundations along any rivers." Faced with the best deal since the Louisiana Purchase, Hoover failed to grasp the free hand from across the sea. From Hamburg, Germany, Richard Wallis, "an expert hydraulic engineer," wanted "to submit to your excellency my judgment and suggestion with a view to canalizing the stream in such manner that devastations such as have visited that region, shall never occur again."

The blueprints piled up, and Hoover's staff, already beset by the problem of administering flood relief, answered the queries as best they could. "Your suggestion is appreciated," began the typical reply, "and I want to assure you that the practicability of all plans will be given due consideration."

Other would-be engineers showed a distrust of the federal government, but they were willing to send in their plans for flood control if they would share in the profits. "If I submit a plan, that is accepted by the government and put in use," wrote one inventor, "will I be entitled to compensation for it?"

Richard Edmonds, a friend of Hoover's and editor of the *Manufacturer's Record* in Baltimore, sent along a letter of introduction for an engineer who had impressed him. Hoover's secretary acknowledged it but added, "You will understand, however, that there are about five hundred people in the United States, each of whom has a new plan for solving the flood control problem."

The five hundred could have saved themselves the trouble had they heeded the jeremiad of Judge L. C. Smith of De Witt, Arkansas. He entitled his pamphlet, "We Should not Meddle with God's Business," and warned that "God never intended that we should levee the Mississippi River, or any of its tributaries, and this you will never do or accomplish. . . . Our government is simply gone to the dogs. I was born on the Arkansas River, and until we commenced to build levees we never did fail to make a crop."[15]

146

A cartoon from the Philadelphia *Ledger,* May 3, 1927. (Red Cross)

In the winter Congress began hearings on flood control, and many people from the flooded area trekked to Washington to tell about the failings of the "levees only" plan. "The disaster of 1927 is not, with those people, a past disaster," LeRoy Percy of Greenville told the committee on January 25, 1928. "They are living under the shadow of it every day and hour. . . . In the flooded area to-day, 10 months after the beginning of the flood, and more than 7 months after the subsidence of it, 20,000 people are carried on the bread list of the Red Cross organization, 5,000 in this territory from which I come."[16]

The hearings revealed how incredibly little engineers knew about flood control. They did not know, for example, whether reservoirs would be effective—because they had never tried such a project, nor even studied it. A colonel from the Corps of Engineers, an expert witness who was in charge of a spillway board, demonstrated this ignorance when he admitted that he did not know exactly what a blue hole was. "I never understood just what the etymology of that was," he admitted. "They usually spell it b-l-e-w, I think. It referred to a water hole there, or at least I thought it referred to a water hole."[17] Yet almost any inhabitant of the flooded area

A cartoon from the St. Louis *Post-Dispatch*, May 17, 1927. Citizens of the valley hoped that Uncle Sam would aid them in keeping the river off the land, even if he did not help them directly during the flood. (Red Cross)

could have told the colonel that it was a b-l-u-e hole because the water usually turned blue, and that it was the hole, some fifty to a hundred feet in depth, which was left when a crevasse gouged out the earth.

Inhabitants of the valley were the most informative witnesses, for they were determined to prevent future floods from destroying their homes and crops. Witness after witness testified before the committee, and they all made one major request—that the federal government take over the financing and planning of flood control. The local levee boards were bankrupt, and the levees would remain broken if left to them. "We do not come as mendicants, we come not as beggars," Judge Percy Bell of Greenville said. "We come as American citizens who are facing a terrific emergency, who need the help of other Americans, and who feel that they are entitled to it and are confident they are going to get it;

and that is the spirit in which we come."[18]

In the end Congress considered two plans, the Jadwin plan, named for the Chief of Engineers, and the Mississippi River Commission plan. The Mississippi River Commission had been established in 1879 and had consistently supported a "levees only" plan of flood control, arguing that spillways, diversion channels, and reservoirs were not capable of taming the river. The House of Representatives Flood Control Committee made a scathing analysis of the Commission's history.

"The result of this policy is now part of the tragic history of flood control in the lower Mississippi in our own time," the report began. "Five devastating epochal floods have visited the valley since the establishment of the commission. On the crest of each, millions of dollars of property have been borne to the sea. Countless thousands of patient, toiling people have been driven from their homes." It enumerated the floods and then noted that flood control experts had urged the Commission to change its narrow concept of control, but the Commission had continually insisted that the levees be built ever higher. "Then came the flood of 1927 and the commission confessed its policy to have been a mistaken one and that not only did the river need levees but additional outlets as well to discharge its flood capacity."

Yet the Commission had already spent $170,000,000 of local taxpayers' money and $71,000,000 of federal money. "It has been described as the monumental blunder of the age, as a policy stubbornly supported in the face of the most convincing opposition, a policy which led the way to tragedy and disaster over the advice of thoughtful and studious men." Not only had the Commission not taken the correct course in flood control; in addition, when Congress called for a recommendation on flood control, it seemed quite reluctant to recommend anything at all. General Edgar Jadwin testified that he had "to prod the Mississippi River Commission to get a definite and constructive recommendation from them. And when their plan came," he complained, "it was full of holes."[19]

Both the Jadwin and the Mississippi River Commission plans included provisions for spillways in addition

149

Although Congress passed a comprehensive plan of flood control in 1928, the first order of business after the river left the flooded land was to rebuild the levees. Workers patching up the levee at Melville, Louisiana. (Louisiana Dept. of Public Works)

to raising the levees and strengthening the crumbling banks. On May 15, 1928, Congress passed a flood control act, appropriating $325,000,000 for construction of a flood control system. The people along the river were gratified to learn that the plan put the expense of construction on the federal government, while the local residents would acquire the rights-of-way and do the maintenance work after the levees were completed. The system of flood control inaugurated in 1928 has served the valley well, and engineers have continually modified the system as the river has tested each plan.[20]

Thus the Mississippi River found its way to the Gulf, reclaiming its flood plain and devastating the settlements that had grown in the shadow of the levees. The gapped levees epitomized an inadequate engineering policy, but the mud-covered land, the askew and high-water-marked buildings, and the million refugees signified even more. The flood was another chapter in the struggle between nature and technology. The levees had caged the river, but at the same time had caused it to rise dangerously high above the land before breaking out; the levees had actually intensified the river's destructive force. On the other hand, advances in communication and transportation, the telegraph, telephone, railroad, motorboat, and automobile, had spared many people from even greater suffering—or death. In retrospect there seems to have been parity between the river and those who lived beside it; neither could claim a complete victory. The river settled back within its banks, and the refugees returned to the land to risk again their fortunes, while engineers opened a new offensive to control floods.

The struggle went on, and perhaps that is the way people preferred it. Through it all, crevasse, rescue, and the long days huddling in the relief camps, refugees often reflected on the river that had driven them from home. Yet none of the documents they left reveals anger at the Mississippi itself; no curses were hurled at it for flooding. People might indeed curse God for allowing the river to run amuck, or damn the engineers whose promises failed—but never the river. The people who lived along the river had respect for it and were in awe of it, and in a real sense they were proud of it. It was as if they expected as much from the Mississippi, for the flood proved once again that the Indians were right with their name—the Father of Waters. The respect that bordered on worship brings to mind a line written by a man who grew up along the river, in the Delta. The people there "fear God and the Mississippi River."[21]

Notes

Chapter 1

[1] *Annual Report of the Chief of Engineers,* United States Army, 1926, "Mississippi River Commission," p. 1793; Mark Twain, *Life on the Mississippi* (New York, 1965, paper), p. 145.

[2] William Faulkner, *Three Famous Short Novels,* "The Old Man" (New York, 1961, paper), pp. 115-16.

[3] Vicksburg *Evening Post,* Apr. 23, 1974; *Weather Bureau Reports,* p. 46, "Relief Work," Commerce Papers, Box 435, Herbert Hoover Presidential Library, West Branch, Iowa (hereafter cited as Hoover Library).

[4] Memphis *Commercial Appeal,* Apr. 10, 12, 17, 1927.

[5] All statistics on flood losses, Red Cross workers, and general factual material not cited otherwise comes from *The Mississippi Valley Flood Disaster of 1927* (Washington, D.C., 1928), the official Red Cross report.

Chapter 2

[1] Alexander Gallatin Paxton, *Three Wars and a Flood* (n.p., n.d.), p. 24; copy in Mississippi Levee Commissioners Office, Greenville.

[2] Interview with Cora Lee Campbell, Greenville, May 17, 1975.

[3] T. H. "Buck" Pryor to Mississippi Educational Television, Apr. 25, 1974; in possession of Henry Kline II, Mississippi Educational Television Network, Jackson.

[4] Louise Henry Cowan, "Overflow in Greenville, 1927," Louise Henry Cowan Papers, William Alexander Percy Library, Greenville; interview with Edwin Bagley, Greenville, May 21, 1975.

[5] Fred Chaney, "A Refugee's Story," Fred Chaney Papers, Mississippi Department of Archives and History, Jackson.

[6] Paxton, *Three Wars,* p. 24; Camden (Ark.) *Evening News,* May 2, 1927.

[7] Memphis *Commercial Appeal,* Apr. 30, 1927.

[8] Cowan, "Overflow in Greenville, 1927."

[9] Interview with William Cobb, Back Gate, Ark., May 25, 1975.

[10] Interview with Robert Murphy, Back Gate, Ark., May 25, 1975.

[11] Interview with Jesse L. Gray, Back Gate, Ark., May 25, 1975.

[12] William Cobb, interview.

[13] Henry Thane to John E. Martineau, Apr. 27, 1927, in John E. Martineau Papers, Arkansas History Commission, Little Rock; interview with C. D. Dupree, Watson, Ark., May 23, 1975.

[14] Interview with Verna Reitzammer, Arkansas City, Ark., May 23, 1975.

[15] Interview with Rocky Reitzammer, Arkansas City, Ark., May 23, 1975.

[16] Verna Reitzammer, interview.

[17] Jesse L. Gray, interview.

[18] Lula Toler, "Flood Relief Work in Jefferson County," (n.d.); "Floods," Department of Agriculture, NA, RG 16.

[19] Interview with Lucyle Cantley, Pine Bluff, Ark., May 26, 1975.

[20] Interview with E. C. Woodyear, Mound, La., May 30, 1975.

[21] Interview with Tucker Couvillon, Marksville, La., June 3, 1975.

[22] Memphis *Commercial Appeal*, May 18, 1927.

[23] Isaac Monroe Cline, *Storms, Floods and Sunshine, A Book of Memoirs* (New Orleans, 1945), pp. 217-18.

[24] Lafayette *Daily Advertiser*, June 10, 1927.

[25] Interview with A. Lewis Bernard, New Iberia, La., June 4, 1975.

[26] Interview with Myrtle Turner Staples, New Iberia, La., June 5, 1975; Staples to author, Sept. 1, 1975.

[27] George W. Healy, Jr., "A Newsman Who Covered It Recalls the Drama of the 1927 Flood," *Dixie*, May 6, 1962, clipping in Louisiana State Library, Baton Rouge.

[28] Ibid.

[29] Vicksburg *Evening Post*, May 4, 1927.

Chapter 3

[1] *Red Cross Courier*, May 1, 1928, p. 15.

[2] The biographical material on Herbert Hoover is general knowledge. For information on Fieser, see Red Cross National Headquarters, Biographical File.

[3] Interview with Herman Caillouet, Greenville, Miss., May 22, 1975.

[4] Interview with Joe Simmons, Metcalfe, Miss., May 17, 1975.

[5] Herman Caillouet, interview.

[6] Interview with Virginia Montgomery Pullen, Vicksburg, Miss., May 12, 1975.

[7] See Greenville *Democratic Times*, Apr. 21, 1927.

[8] Interview with Frank Hall, Greenville, Miss., May 22, 1975.

[9] John E. Montgomery to author, Feb. 13, 1976.

[10] Vicksburg *Evening Post*, May 12, June 15, 1927.

[11] Memphis *Commercial Appeal*, Apr. 24, 1927.

[12] Interview with E. J. Smith, Greenville, Miss., May 21, 1975; U.S. Congress, House, Flood Control Committee, *Hearings,* Testimony of A. H. Blaess, Nov. 8, 1927, 70th Cong., 1st sess., 1927, pt. 1; *Bulletin of the American Railway Engineers Association,* "The Mississippi Valley Flood—1927," 29 (July 1927), 58, copy in Mississippi River Commission Library, Vicksburg.

[13] Camden *Evening News*, May 2, 1927; Memphis *Commercial Appeal*, Apr. 24, 1927; Vicksburg *Evening Post,* May 4, 1927.

[14] Memphis *Commercial Appeal*, Apr. 30, 1927.

[15] Interview with Eric Hardy, Monticello, Ark., May 24, 1975.

[16] Memphis *Commercial Appeal*, Apr. 26, 1927.

[17] Ibid. May 16, 1927.

[18] Report of Lieutenant W. D. Sample, "Use of Naval Planes and Personnel During Mississippi River Flood Emergency of 1927," July 1, 1927, Commerce Papers, "Mississippi Valley Flood Relief Work," Box 423, Hoover Library.

[19] Interview with Victor Bobb, Vicksburg, May 12, 1975.

[20] H. S. Browne, Jr., "Remark Sheet, Mississippi Flood Relief, U.S. Coast Guard, 1927, *Saukee*," June 10, 1927, Records of U.S. Coast Guard, Box 2020, NA, RG 26.

[21] *Red Cross Courier*, June 15, 1927.

[22] M. W. Rasmussen, "Coast Guard Activities, Mississippi River Flood, April, May and June 1927," Sept. 6, 1927, Records of U.S. Coast Guard, Box 2020, NA, RG 26.

[23] H. S. Browne, Jr., "Remark Sheet, Mississippi Flood Relief, U.S. Coast Guard, 1927, *Saukee*," June 10, 1927, ibid.

[24] Ibid.

[25] "Report Sheet, Mississippi Flood Relief, 1927" (n.d.), ibid.

[26] H. H. Wolf, "Mississippi Flood Relief, Final Report," June 16, 1927, ibid.

[27] Virginia Montgomery Pullen, interview.

Chapter 4

[1] Interview with Cora Lee Campbell, Greenville, May 17, 1975; Interview with Verna Reitzammer, Arkansas City, May 23, 1975.

[2] Herbert Hoover, Radio Address, May 28, 1927, "Relief Work, Reports, Statements, Press Releases," Box 432, Commerce Papers, Hoover Library; DeWitt Smith to Hoover, Jan. 31, 1928, "Mississippi Valley Flood Relief Work, Hearings," Commerce Papers, ibid. For a specific report of the *Pelican* disaster, see material in U.S. Corps of Engineers Memphis District, Main File, Records Section M 37, "High Water," Corps of Engineers Office, Memphis. Documents in the Red Cross Archives show that, according to what officials admitted were incomplete reports, of the 443 people who died during the flood, 237 drowned—78 in Arkansas, 125 in Mississippi, and 16 in Louisiana. All of those in Louisiana and certainly many in Arkansas and Mississippi drowned after Hoover and the Red Cross took over rescue coordination. See "List of Persons Drowned and Death by Diseases," "Deaths from Drowning Due to Flood," May 23, June 6, 1927, file 224.6201, Red Cross Archives, Washington, D.C. (hereafter cited as Red Cross Archives). Newspapers also document the drownings. In addition to Memphis *Commercial Appeal*, Apr. 24-30, see Monroe (La.) *News-Star*, May 16, 1927; Pine Bluff (Ark.) *Daily Graphic*, Apr. 29, 1927; Lafayette (La.) *Daily Advertiser*, July 8, 1927, and Jackson (Miss.) *Clarion Ledger*, Apr. 30, May 6, 1927.

[3] Mrs. Waggaman Berl, "What Easter Brought from up our Majestic River," *Red Cross Courier*, July 15, 1927, pp. 6-7.

[4] R. S. Wilson, "Rehabilitation Work by Extension Department," ACC 702, DR 183, Records of the Federal Extension Service, NA, RG 33.

[5] Ibid.

[6] Interview with Virginia Montgomery Pullen, Vicksburg, May 12, 1975.

[7] Lugenia B. Christmas, "Flood Work in St. Francis Co." (n.d.), Records of the Office of the Secretary of Agriculture, NA, RG 16.

[8] Interview with Maude Maddox, Arkansas City, May 24, 1975.

[9] Dora S. Stubblefield, "Refugee Work, Craighead County" (n.d.), Records of the Office of the Secretary of Agriculture, NA, RG 16.

[10] Geraldine Green Orrell, "Home Demonstration Work Done with Flood Sufferers, Poinsett Co." (n.d.), ibid.

[11] Interview with Albert Tilbury, Chemin-A-Haut Park, La., June 1, 1975.

[12] Memphis *Commercial Appeal*, May 6, 1927; Report of Thomas M. Campbell (n.d.), Robert R. Moton Papers, Tuskegee Institute Archives, Tuskegee Institute, Ala., Box GC 48 (hereafter cited as Moton Papers). See in Box GC 48 the entire unpublished report of the Colored Advisory Commission. A copy is also in the Red Cross Archives. Cora Lee Campbell, interview. For a complete account of peonage during the flood, see Pete Daniel, *The Shadow of Slavery: Peonage in the South, 1901-1969* (Urbana, 1972), pp. 149-69.

[13] Thomas M. Campbell (n.d.), GC 48, Moton Papers.

[14] Unpublished report of the Colored Advisory Commission, ibid.

[15] Baker to McClintock, May 10; DeWitt Smith to Baker, May 15; J. A. Hendrix to Richardson, May 19; Baker to Hendrix, May 27; Leonard G. Coop to Baker, June 6; A. C. Bowman to Coop, June 7; Baker to Coop, June 10, 1927, Disaster Relief File 224.43, "The Mississippi Flood of 1927," Red Cross Archives.

[16] Frederick Simpich, "The Great Mississippi Flood of 1927," *National Geographic* 52 (Sept. 1927), 265.

[17] Memphis *Commercial Appeal*, May 16, 1927.

[18] Ibid. Apr. 25, 1927.

[19] Ibid.; *The Baptist and Commoner*, May 4, 1927.

[20] Lafayette *Daily Advertiser*, May 28, June 27, 1927; Memphis *Commercial Appeal*, May 15, 1927. While Cajun is not broken French, it is a distinctive form of French.

[21] Maude Chambers to Mary Jessie Stone (n.d., 1927), ACC 702, DR 183, Records of the Federal Extension Service, NA, RG 33.

[22] Valeria Parker to William R. Redden, Weekly Report, June 9-17, 1927; Margaret Wells Wood to Parker, June 25, 1927, Disaster Relief File, 224.5, Red Cross Archives.

[23] Albert Read, Report, June 20, 1927, ibid.

[24] Read, Weekly Report, July 10-20, 1927, ibid.

[25] Read, Reports, June 16, 18, 1927, Parker to Redden, June 9, 1927, ibid.

[26] Wood, Report, June 20, 1927, ibid.

[27] Wood to Parker, June 20, July 10, 1927, ibid.

[28] Redden to Parker, Oct. 17, 1927, ibid.

[29] Wood to Parker, July 10, 1927, ibid.

Chapter 5

[1] Lafayette *Daily Advertiser,* June 18, 1927; Margaret Wells Wood to Valeria Parker, July 10, 1927, Disaster Relief File, 224.5, Red Cross Archives.

[2] F. H. Deverto to John McMullen, July 16, 1927, "Mississippi Valley Flood Relief Work, Rehabilitation," Box 430, Commerce Papers, Hoover Library.

[3] Interview with Mrs. E. J. Smith, Greenville, May 21, 1975; E. E. Bass to Herman Solomon, June 8, 1927, copies in U.S. Army Corps of Engineers District Headquarters, Vicksburg, and in Mississippi Levee Commissioners Office, Greenville; Interview with Cora Lee Campbell, Greenville, May 17, 1975.

[4] Memphis *Commercial Appeal,* May 6, 1927.

[5] T. Roy Reid to C. L. Thompson, July 21, 1927, Box 429, Commerce Papers, Hoover Library.

[6] Herbert Hoover, Radio Address, May 28, 1927, "Relief Work, Reports, Statements, Press Releases," Box 432, Commerce Papers, Hoover Library.

[7] Turner Catledge, Interview, Oral History Collection; Hoover to Louis Pearson, May 26, 1927, "Mississippi Valley Relief Work," Box 429, ibid.

[8] O. J. Hill to John E. Martineau, June 6, 1927, John E. Martineau Papers, Arkansas History Commission, Little Rock.

[9] E. T. Cashion to Martineau, June 18, 1927, ibid.

[10] Mrs. Bird Tatum, "Flood Report" (n.d.), Records of the Office of the Secretary of Agriculture, NA, RG 16.

[11] Frank M. Heath, *Forty Million Hoofbeats: Factual Story of the 11,356 Mile Trip of Gypsy Queen under Saddle* (New York, 1941), p. 377.

[12] Moton to Hoover, June 13, 1927, GC 48, Moton Papers.

[13] Griffin to Clark, Nov. 6, 1927, Disaster Relief File, 224.91/08, Red Cross Archives.

[14] Fieser to DeWitt Smith, Dec. 19, 1927; Robert R. Moton, "Summary of Report of Colored Advisory Commission on Flood Relief Following Inspection Tour of December 1927," Disaster Relief File, 224.91/08, Red Cross Archives; Hoover to Moton, Dec. 16, 1927, GC 37, Moton Papers; *The Final Report of the Colored Advisory Commission* (Washington, D.C., 1929).

[15] A. C. Jones to Hoover, Aug. 15, Box 425; J. McClean to Hoover, May 22, Box 426; Sidney V. Lowell to Hoover, Nov. 11, Box 427; Story B. Ladd to Hoover, Apr. 27, May 4, Box 427; C. E. Eacrett to Hoover, July 14, 1927, Box 424, "Mississippi Valley Flood Relief Work, Plans," Commerce Papers, Hoover Library; U.S. Congress, House, Flood Control Committee, *Hearings,* Statement of Frank Fredeen, Jan. 17, 70th Cong., 1st sess., 1928; F. E. Muratet to Hoover, May 27, Box 426; J. W. Hamilton to Hoover, May 26, Box 424; Elmer Robinson to Hoover, July 29, Box 427; I. E. Officer to Hoover, Aug. 31, Box 426; "A Citizen" to Hoover, May 6, Box 424; Vladimir Skrivauck to Hoover, July 16, Box 426; M. M. D. Vituac Company to Hoover, June 8, Box 427; Richard Wallis to Hoover, May 8, Box 427; see numerous replies in Boxes 424-27; B. F. Canady to Hoover, Aug.

14, Box 424; Akerson to Edmonds, July 7, Box 424; L. C. Smith to Hoover, June 27, 1927, Box 427, "Mississippi Valley Flood Relief Work, Plans," Commerce Papers, Hoover Library; Monroe (La.) *News-Star*, May 16, 1927.

[16] U.S. Congress, House, Commerce Committee, *Hearings*, "Flood Control," 70th Cong., 1st sess., 1928, p. 99.

[17] U.S. Congress, House, Flood Control Committee, *Hearings*, Testimony of Colonel William P. Wooten, Dec. 15, 1927, 70th Cong., 1st sess., 1927, pt. 3, p. 1955.

[18] Statement of Judge Percy Bell, pt. 1, p. 1927, ibid.

[19] "Flood Control on the Mississippi River," pp. 83-84; Testimony of General Edgar Jadwin, p. 4379, ibid.

[20] U.S. Army Corps of Engineers, *Flood Control; Lower Mississippi Valley* (Vicksburg, 1970) *passim*.

[21] David Lewis Cohn, *Where I Was Born and Raised* (Boston, 1948), p. 43.

Index